Casey Jones Epic Of The American Railroad

CASEY JONES

EPIC OF THE AMERICAN RAILROAD

By

FRED J. LEE

"Come, all you Rounders, I want you to hear
The story told of a brave engineer;
Casey Jones was the Rounder's name,
A high right-wheeler of mighty fame."

(From the original ballad
by WALLACE SAUNDERS.)

SOUTHERN PUBLISHERS, INC.

KINGSPORT   TENNESSEE

MANUFACTURED IN THE UNITED STATES OF AMERICA
KINGSPORT PRESS, INC.   KINGSPORT, TENNESSEE

To All Those Who by Their Vision and Sacrifice
Have Made the Railroad Symbolical of the
Spirit of American Progress and Perseverance
This Book Is Respectfully Dedicated

FOREWORD

MR. FRED J. LEE has given a full and correct account of the life of my husband and his friend, and it has been my pleasure to give him my unreserved cooperation and direct assistance in the preparation of the book *Casey Jones*.

I have received many curious inquiries from all over the world and have taken part in numerous ceremonies, radio programs and dedicatory exercises in honor of my beloved husband. My chief purpose in the latter years of my life is to tell the world in every way I can how wonderfully he deserved every honor bestowed upon him in life and every honor accorded his memory since his death. I do not know as well as some his superior qualifications as a locomotive engineer for which he became so celebrated, but I do know that in personality, character and disposition he had no superior.

It is my belief that this volume and the monument at Cayce, Kentucky, sponsored by the Hickman, Kentucky, Lions Club and dedicated by Senator Alben Barkley to his memory in 1938 will be, throughout the years to come, the true permanent memorials to Casey Jones.

Sincerely

Mrs Casey Jones

v

INTRODUCTION

THERE is a wide difference between the saturated steam locomotives of the late nineteenth century and the sleek aluminum, streamlined Diesel and electric engines of today capable of developing speeds up to two hundred miles per hour, but the technique, methods and personalities of the earlier romantic period comprise an essentially important and extremely interesting chapter in the history of the American railroad.

From the vast army of workers who were responsible for the actual operation and maintenance of the railroad in the nineties one name has arisen that will survive in memory as long as the railroad in any form exists. It radiates the spirit of romance and adventure inherent in the American railroad.

That name is Casey Jones.

There must be some fundamental vital element in any ballad that is accepted as a folk song. The element assumes additional weight and significance when the hero of the ballad was a real living human being. It was such a person who inspired the song that has been sung around the world.

The author has gone to every known available source in order that historical accuracy might be preserved, and has spared no pains to follow every clew that promised to throw light upon the life of Casey

Jones, the man. Whenever possible, every story concerning him has been verified, and nothing of doubtful authenticity has been retained.

An exact chronology has been followed, and although the story is told in fictional form care has been taken not to color the related incidents more than the known facts warranted. The purpose has been to recreate the scenes and make them live again. Most of the characters are or were real persons, with whose names no liberties have been taken. It is only when names have been forgotten and no known record of them was to be found that fictitious names have been substituted.

To avoid retarding the narrative more than the author believed was necessary to a clear understanding of certain episodes and situations, many pertinent but more or less technical details have been incorporated in an Appendix to which reference is made by suitable footnotes. Subjects of a purely statistical, historical or biographical nature are enlarged upon in the same way.

Accordingly, this volume is offered as a complete story of Casey Jones, hero of the American railroad, presented against a background of the railroad as it was during the period of its most significant growth and development.

Without generous assistance the story never could have been undertaken, much less brought to completion. The author appreciates the help of those who opened their records, who authenticated or disproved supposititious facts, and who supplied much valuable historical data. The author acknowledges indebtedness especially to the following:

Mrs. J. L. Jones of Jackson, Tennessee, widow of Casey Jones; Judge Jack F. White of Clearwater, Florida, formerly of Jackson, Tennessee; Mr. R. E. Edrington, Assistant Grand Chief Engineer, Brotherhood of Locomotive Engineers; Mr. B. J. Feeny, traveling engineer of the Illinois Central Railroad and past-President of the Traveling Engineers Association; Mr. C. R. Young, Superintendent of Transportation, and Mr. C. J. Corliss, Historian, of the Illinois Central System; Mr. William Bosma, of Water Valley, Mississippi, Illinois Central engineer; Mr. B. B. Tolson, Superintendent of the Mobile & Ohio Railroad at Murphysboro, Illinois; Mr. V. J. Thompson, Chief Operating Officer, Mobile & Ohio Railroad, St. Louis, Missouri; Sim T. Webb, Memphis, sometime fireman for Casey Jones; Mr. Claude M. Starke, Chicago; the Canadian Railways Magazine for September, 1932; the following residents of Jackson, Tennessee:

Mr. John R. Gaffney, a retired engineer; Mr. Colie Chandler and Mr. James T. Gaffney, active engineers of the Illinois Central, and Miss Grace Chandler.

THE AUTHOR

CONTENTS

ILLUSTRATIONS

CASEY JONES

CHAPTER I

SCENE BY THE RIVER

CASEY JONES was not the creature of a song-smith's imagination. Nor was he born in a locomotive cab. On the contrary, he was a very real human being and he was born in a region untouched by the railroad. He was christened John Luther Jones.

He came into the world in a remote spot in South-eastern Missouri now impossible to identify, and he was in his thirteenth year when he first saw a steam engine of any kind. Several more years were to elapse before he was to know the thrill of having a "throttle in his hand."

He was fifteen when he was first called "Casey" under circumstances that verged on the tragic for him if amusing to the onlookers. This nickname grew to take the place of his baptismal name until the latter virtually was lost sight of, and it was as "Casey" that the railroad, and later the world, came to know him. It is the name that inspired the song that has been sung and played and whistled 'round the world; a name that is a part of authentic railroad history, the name of one who rose to fame in his calling and met an heroic death at the end of the run.

While he was still a young man a glamour had begun to envelop him that spread his renown far beyond the railroad world, and though he was only in his thirties when he unflinchingly faced death in order that many lives might be spared, his was a career rich in accomplishment.

Today the mention of his name evokes open admiration from his contemporaries, and many who have risen to high positions warmly proclaim him to be their ideal of both Man and Engineer. It is fitting, therefore, that Casey Jones be enshrined in memory as the outstanding hero of the American railroad.

The man himself, his striking appearance and unusual personality, the things that he did and the manner of his doing them, explain why the song, so familiar in every quarter of the globe, came into existence. Judged by critical musical standards, it would be difficult to find any merit in the ballad. It originated in the brain of an illiterate, simple-minded Negro engine wiper, yet it possesses that indefinable spark that keeps it alive through the years.*

John Luther Jones was born on March 14, 1863, in a backwoods region of Southeastern Missouri that cannot be definitely located. His father, Frank Jones, was a poor country school teacher. His mother, Ann Nolen Jones, was a woman of considerable strength of char-

* See Appendix, note 7.

acter, with an innate refinement and a degree of culture that must have made her lot as a pioneer in a backwoods settlement uncommonly hard to endure, though from these same qualities she drew the necessary strength and courage to withstand the hardships of such a life.

Ann Nolen Jones was not the kind of woman to bow meekly to fate, to accept tamely undesirable conditions that spirit and initiative might change for the better. She was ambitious for her family and determined that her children should have more and better opportunities than a wilderness was ever likely to offer; and as a result of her resolution, in September, 1876, the family turned their backs upon their primitive home and emigrated to the western part of Kentucky, settling near the town of Hickman.

John Luther—or simply Luther as he was more generally known in this early period of his life—was the oldest of five children, four boys and one girl. In order, following Luther, the boys were Eugene, Frank and Phillip. Their sister's name was Emma.

The four Jones brothers all became in time engineers on the Illinois Central Railroad. There was also another quartet of brothers, Chandler by name, who likewise became engineers on the same railroad.* And it was decreed that the careers of these two sets of brothers were to be curiously intermingled in the days to come.

There is no purpose on the part of the writer deliberately to inject a vein of mysticism into this chronicle,

* See Appendix, note 13.

because it is, first and last, the true life story of Casey
Jones; his life just as he lived it, citing every pertinent
scrap of information that may help to portray the man
as he was. But this very aim demands that such factors
as, for instance, the interplay of influences between the
four Chandler boys on the one hand and the four Jones
boys on the other, Emma's one exhibition of sinister
clairvoyance, and the extraordinary premonitions of the
little black engine wiper, Wallace Saunders, be accorded
more than passing attention. Each of such details enters
into the very warp and woof of Casey Jones' history.

Two days with one night between were required to
make the journey to Hickman, the means of transportation being two canvas-covered wagons, each drawn by a
span of mules; with Bulger, the flea-bitten hound, trailing dejectedly astern.

If Ann Nolen Jones had not kept a journal, in which
she intermittently confided during these early days,
most of the details of this exodus from Southeastern
Missouri would be lacking. One wagon and its span of
mules belonged to Frank Jones, the other outfit having
been provided by one Tom Billingsby, who accompanied
the family in the capacity of guide and helper.

Illiterate backwoodsman though Tom Billingsby may
have been, Mrs. Jones' journal pays him this tribute:
"We never would have surmounted the difficulties of
the trail without Mr. Billingsby's kind assistance and
expert guidance."

The immediate objective was Bird's Point, a boat

landing on the Missouri side of the river opposite Cairo, Illinois, where the family were to embark with their effects on a steamboat that would deliver them in due course at Hickman.

The most that Bird's Point could boast was the combined general store and dwelling occupied by one David Tuttle and family, and the fact that steamboats now and then put in there to replenish their cordwood fuel supply or to take aboard an infrequent passenger. Today a modern highway bridge spans the river at this point, and on the road maps Bird's Point is spelled as one word, Birdspoint.

The Jones caravan halted at Tuttle's store at twilight, but before dark, of their second day of travel. Across the wide sweep of the Mississippi where the Ohio River joins the larger stream, the gas and oil lamps of Cairo, "over in Egypt," on the southernmost tip of Illinois, were beginning to blink, beckoning them to come across and mocking their inability to do so. A vague white mist swirled slowly above the surface of the waters, rising from and clinging to it, folding and unfolding to form weird, fantastic shapes that dissolved into other shapes no less weird and fantastic. The movement of this vast blanket of vapor was so slow that one did not sense it immediately, but it was constant, and the shadowy shapes at last dissipated into nothingness, merging into the advancing phalanx of night where the eye could not penetrate.

Sounds carried tremendous distances through the

twilight hush. From over yonder, where the lamps were now veiled and now revealed by the coiling mists, came a medley of strange, uncouth noises: a clanking and clattering and banging and puffing and a hissing of escaping steam that was demoniacal to one who never before had heard the like. Occasionally was heard a deeper, more resonant note; a vibrant, bellowing roar that punctuated and became a part of the bedlam. These latter sounds denoted that out there on the waters the huge train ferry, *William H. Osborne,* was plying without rest between Illinois and Kentucky, conveying entire trains across the Ohio River, and that the cargo boats were arriving and departing at Cairo, carrying traffic between that busy river port and Columbus, Kentucky, northern terminal of the Mobile & Ohio Railroad.

The effect of the fog-muffled tumult upon John Luther Jones was immediate. Minutes passed while he stood motionless, gazing out over the river, lips slightly parted in awe and wonder. Then he spoke, breathless with excitement.

"Mr. Billingsby! What's that? What's all those sounds I hear?" Then before the surprised Mr. Billingsby could reply: "Golly! It can't be! . . . Yes—it is! The railroad!"

The man was amazed at the transformed boy.

"Gosh!" he ejaculated to himself. "Did you ever!" And aloud: "Don't have a conniption fit, Bub. 'Course it's the railroad. And the railroad ferry boats, too. The yards are over in Cairo—miles on miles of steel tracks with en-gines a-puffin' an' a-rollin'! An' there's one big ferry boat—a hundred times bigger'n my barn—onto which trains air run and ferried back an' forth 'twixt Illinois and Kentucky." Here the old fellow's amazement suddenly deepened. He voiced his perplexity.

"How do you know it's the railroad? You ain't ever heerd or seen steam cyars or en-gines!"

This was true. Nor could Luther have explained how he knew the sounds that smote his ears emanated from a large and busy railroad yard. Rapt in his own wonderment he was only vaguely aware of the other's bewilderment and he did not try to reply. He stood, trembling with excitement, staring across at the unattainable, completely fascinated. Tom Billingsby helplessly shook his head and turned away.

The other children, in various stages of sleepy fretfulness, were being dragged from their wagon by their parents. Frank Jones was tired and irritable and in no mood to stand any nonsense. He spoke to them impatiently until his wife quietly took charge, bidding him go and make the necessary arrangements with David Tuttle for staying the night.

Incidents seemingly trivial at the time of their occurrence may prove to be of utmost significance in the light of after events. So it was in the case of the episode that next aroused the weary travelers before they could reach the portals of David Tuttle's domicile.

Emma, who was eight and an unimaginative child, was being propelled forward by her mother, who carried the infant Phillip. Emma's knuckles tried to bore the sleep from her eyes, and she whined peevishly. Their general direction, rendered uncertain by the child's wabbling gait, was toward the gallery across the front of the Tuttle establishment, each step bringing them nearer the river's brink.

Suddenly Emma shrank back, colliding violently with her mother's knees, and her childish treble voice shrilled a piercing note of frantic terror. The child was staring wide-eyed into the writhing river vapors. Then she buried her face in her mother's skirts, which, in a measure, muffled her wild outcries. Mrs. Jones, hampered by the baby, looked about helplessly.

The entire company was puzzled and alarmed. Even Luther was jarred from his absorption. The pedagogue's irritation flared up in an outburst.

"Good Lord, Mother! What's the matter with that child? Has she gone crazy?"

"Don't shout at me," sharply from Ann. "Come get Phillip. . . . I don't know what's the matter with her."

Phillip had reacted to the commotion with a lusty wailing of his own, which was intensified after he was transferred to his father's arms.

Then Emma's cries ceased as abruptly as they had begun, and she became utterly silent. But terror lingered in her eyes. Twilight was blending into darkness. Across the river the lights, when not veiled by the mists,

By the River

sparkled more brightly. A measure of calm was restored, but despite her coaxing and tender caresses Ann Nolen could not get a coherent word from Emma to explain her conduct. Something—something strange and dreadful that no other eye had seen—some weird vision out there amid the swirling river mists—had stricken the little girl dumb.

Some time later, after darkness had fallen, Frank Jones missed his eldest son.

"Where's Luther?" he inquired.

Old Tom Billingsby answered, guiltily, "Last I see him he's out yonder moonin' on the river bank."

The pedagogue stormed: "What in the world is possessing the children tonight?"—and strode outside as if hoping to find an answer there.

Luther did not stir, did not so much as hear his exasperated sire, until his right ear was firmly grasped between a determined thumb and forefinger. Rudely he was twisted round and his father commanded:

"Get yourself inside the house, young man. March!"

CHAPTER II

PASTURES NEW—THE WATER TANK

L UTHER'S first view of the Mississippi, at dusk,
disclosed to him the kind of phantasmagoria that
sinks deep into the impressionable mind of a boy. The
ghostly blanket of vapor, eddying ceaselessly, by turns
opened up to reveal and then closed to conceal the lights
of Cairo, where every fiber of him yearned to be. His
excited senses saw strange, fantastic shapes in that far-
flung winding sheet of fog, and he felt that he was
being offered and then denied a revelation of wonderful
things yet to come.

Certainly there were distinct differences between the
experiences of Emma and Luther upon their first
glimpse of the river. But from that night there existed
between brother and sister a certain bond of sympathy,
very real if not always apparent, that lasted throughout
their lives.

Emma's panic was soon forgotten by her parents, but
it stuck in the back of Luther's mind. When a long
procession of mileposts came rushing at Casey Jones
out of the murky mists of a fog-enshrouded dawn, their
spectral outlines awoke a chord of memory and vividly
renewed the scene by the river.

Oddly enough, Luther retained only a hazy recollec-

tion of the last leg of their journey. Since none of the
boys had ever seen a steam engine of any kind, one
would expect that Luther at least would have remembered clearly some of the details of the machinery
that propelled the dingy old side-wheeler, *The New
Mary Houston*, which picked up the Jones family and
their belongings at Bird's Point and deposited them,
ultimately, at Hickman. But this, apparently, did not
impress him greatly. Luther was a sensitive youngster,
and it seems that he was more acutely affected by the
ridiculous appearance of the battered old tub, whose
very name took on a derisive implication. When a *new*,
gleaming-white St. Louis-New Orleans packet, stately
and palatial, overhauled and steamed past them, it made
their own boat's dinginess appear more pronounced by
contrast, made her seem even more ancient and disrep-
utable.

From Bird's Point to Hickman the distance is not
great, but *The New Mary Houston*, zigzagging back
and forth across the river to halt at numerous landings,
required all of a day to cover this last lap of their
journey. She might have been the Irish Mail of the
river, like the mixed freight and passenger trains that
acknowledged every flag-stop. Certainly she bore no
resemblance to the proud packets that swept up and
down the river, tieing up only at the more important
stops.

The family's final destination was the tiny village of
Cayce, some nine miles inland from Hickman. They

were soon comfortably settled there, enjoying a hum-
drum existence. The pedagogue presided over the
rural school, of which three of the boys and Emma became average pupils. Ann Jones attended to the infant
Phillip and to her household duties, and now and then
found time to devote to her journal.

During the ensuing two years some things happened,
however, that produced in Ann Jones a vague un-
easiness about her boy, John Luther. The causes were
to be found no farther away than the Water Tank of
the Mobile & Ohio Railroad which, with the little station, telegraph office and one long passing track, denoted
the railroad's existence to the village of Cayce.

From a scenic standpoint the vicinity of the Water
Tank was as uninviting as one could imagine. Round
about was a scanty growth of weeds, mostly ragweeds
and jimson weeds, which found a precarious rooting
among the blistering cinders and provided cover for a
strident chorus of insects. The tank itself, beneath
whose hinged spout a freight locomotive now and then
stopped to fill the tank of its tender, was so old and
sodden and so covered with slime and green moss that
it was remarkable how the rusty iron hoops held it
together. Through countless leaks in its rotting seams
water perpetually dripped to form greasy, black puddles
in the cinders: a festering spot during the long, hot
summer days and nights. But for Luther and some of
the other boys the whole place was a realm of magic.

Impressions acquired at the Water Tank stayed with

Luther through life. Every train that roared past the village, or that paused briefly, was an event. His boyish imagination was obsessed. Ann Jones began to realize the changes that were taking place, perceiving to some extent the factors that were influencing her first born—and she became suspicious, then resentful of conditions beyond her power to control.

More and more she observed that Luther's adventures at the Water Tank were kindling an ambition which she viewed with the liveliest misgivings. And like innumerable mothers before and since, when confronted with similar problems, there was nothing she could do about it.

The Water Tank unquestionably symbolizes the period of Luther Jones' life in which his future was being shaped. Many of the things that happened there were among the most vivid recollections of his later years. And although a visit to the scene, many years after, was disillusioning, as such returns generally are, a fascination hung about it that still enthralled him.

Of this formative period in the life of Luther Jones there were some two years, bringing him to the ripe age of fifteen. He saw less and less of school as he became increasingly occupied with more directly practical matters, and soon his formal schooling ended entirely.

But Luther was storing up a fund of knowledge outside the classrooms. On one occasion—it was a bright, clear day in late winter—he journeyed to the Water Tank to make his usual observations. The ice was be-

Station at Cayce, Kentucky

ginning to thaw and fall in odd-shaped pieces from the sides and rims of the big spout and cylinder. In the glistening sunlight it presented a fascinating picture. The trainmen would be happy, thought Luther, now that the dangers and disadvantages of the cold winter months would soon be past.

The boy somehow felt that he was being noticed more and more by the members of the train crews that stopped here. His burning curiosity was bound to attract their notice in time, but he would have been astonished to know how word of it had already spread along the division and how often his avid interest was made a topic of comment.

On this occasion Luther addressed a certain fireman, Steve Gowdy by name, who had paused in his task of cleaning his fire to consider the boy. Steve's face carried a slightly puzzled look as he gazed at Luther. Steve thought, "It's a long, long time since *I* was as green as that kid!"

The boy had to overcome a painful shyness to timidly ask: "Why does steam squirt from them spigots when you-all start to slow down?"

The engineer, applying the spout of his tallowpot to the rod cups, turned to survey Luther and chuckle at the ingenious question.

"Spigots!" the fireboy exploded. "What the hell do you mean?"

In a low aside, the engineer explained: "He means the cylinder cocks."

The fireman tossed back his head and laughed uproariously. One would think he had never heard anything half so funny. Hugging the handle end of the slice bar under one arm, he wiped his eyes on the back of a grimy leather gauntlet, an operation that resulted in adding more soot to an already blackened face.

"By God, that's good!" he managed to get out at length. "Wait till I tell the fellas that! You heard him, Bill! He said 'spigots,' didn't he? Haw! Haw! Spigots!"

Luther was overcome with embarrassment. His innocent question had tickled the risibilities of this lordly engine crew—all engine crews were a race of superior beings to Luther—and drove home forcibly how green he really was. But, then, how was a fella ever to learn anything if he didn't ask questions?

Possibly that would have been the end of the incident if the engineer had not intervened. He glanced again at the boy. Underneath an agony of mortification, he discerned an earnestness of purpose that was not forever going to be turned aside by harsh banter. The day was coming when that boy could pass it back as hard as ever it would be handed to him!

He spoke to his fireboy again: "You once were as green as he is, Steve."

Steve's contemptuous snort had the effect of catching the charge in mid-air and hurling it from him with violent scorn.

"Me? Good God'll mighty, nobody was ever that

green! Why, me, I was brung up sucking a petcock
'stead of a nipple." Once more he eyed Luther, trying
to classify him. By and by he vouchsafed:

"Kid, them ain't spigots—them's cylinder cocks. And
this here old mudhen squirts steam when she slows
down 'cause she's chuck full of beans."

Luther let it go at that—for the time being—but out
of the episode grew a resolve never again to lay himself
open to the ridicule of anybody as wise and great as a
locomotive fireman. Particularly, Steve. Rough,
tough, blasphemous, hard-drinking, good-natured Steve
Gowdy.

About this time he found in the school's meager li-
brary a dog-eared book on mechanical engineering. Its
cover and title page and many others of its pages were
missing; but if any one thing were needed to prove that
Luther Jones was born to become a locomotive engineer,
it was the clarity, amounting to intuition, with which he
assimilated what this volume had to impart. More
than that, without any means at hand for practical ex-
perimentation, the mechanical side of his brain supplied
inductively much that the old opus did not touch or en-
large upon. Luther literally wore out the dilapidated
volume, which, apparently, was never missed from its
place on the shelf. What with the book and the persistent catechism to which he subjected the various engine
crews, he stored up an amazing wealth of information
about steam locomotives.

Another day, months later, he stood watching No. 22

—with fuller understanding now—as she slowed down
to take water at the Water Tank. No. 22 was one of
the regular northbound freights, and she stopped daily
for water. Her drawing to a stop had become an intensely interesting proceeding for Luther because he
understood it better. There were no brakes of any description on the locomotive, a lumbering old broad-
gauge machine, and the cars were equipped only with
hand brakes. A stop that would halt the manhole of
the tender tank directly under the big hinged spout,
which was swung downward, depended almost entirely
upon the engineer's skill. Just how Luther had
gathered together and read correctly all the various
mechanical angles that made the operation understand-
able to him it would be impossible to say, but the fact
remains that he did know. He had, too, picked up the
knowledge that "mudhen" was a familiar name by which
the saturated-steam type of locomotive of that era was
identified by those who worked with them.

Luther could tell when the Johnson-bar was dragged
into reverse position, and could gauge by the steam jets
gushing from the open cylinder cocks precisely how
much steam was being fed to pull her down without
ripping out her piston packings. As often as not, he had
observed, engines ran by the Water Tank—sometimes
as much as a train length—and had to back up if they
wanted to take on water. This meant that the timing
and teamwork between train and engine crews were not
so good; the profanely heated exchanges between the

two crews, when the halt was finally made, attested to the truth of this.

But, today, the engineer was not going to allow his drag to run by the Water Tank; he was making a good job of the stop. The big spout dipped squarely over the manhole.

In the fireman, still panting from his exertions with the unwieldy Johnson-bar, Luther recognized his old acquaintance, Steve Gowdy. Steve squatted, half exhausted, on the manhole cover while the water poured into the tank with a prodigious splash and gurgle. As he recovered his breath, he eyed the grinning youngster, and a glint of recognition came into his eyes.

"Hi-yeh," Luther sounded a polite greeting. And Steve returned, after a suitable pause:

"Hi-yeh, Spigots. Whatcha grinning at? See anything green?"

"Yeh," said the boy. "Sprouting up there on the manhole lid." And he was emboldened to add: "Try some of them beans you been feeding your old mudhen and maybe you won't get all scruffed pulling her into reverse."

The engineer, climbing down with the inevitable tallowpot, paused to laugh appreciatively, then proceeded with his work.

Steve stared.

"Is that so! Somebody's pretty damn smart all of a sudden, ain't they?" He felt it necessary to explain to his engineer: "Less'n a year ago this here bean pole

didn't know what a cylinder cock is; now he's ready to
run a engine." And again to Luther:

"You'd bust your main gut if you ever rassled a
Johnson-bar."

"Huh!" Luther was broadly contemptuous. "I
betcha I can pull your old Johnson-bar over without
getting the heaves, anyhow." Which fetched another
laugh from the engineer.

This was pure braggadocio, of course; he had never
so much as laid a hand upon the murderous piece of
mechanism, source of unnumbered casualties in the
engine cab; but it showed that he was gaining a measure
of self-confidence, and was not to be bluffed, even by
the lordly Steve.

That Steve recognized, in some measure, this change
of attitude on the part of the greenhorn was indicated
by his own abrupt change of front.

"Kid," said he, "how about cleaning my fire for me?"

But the engineer forestalled acceptance of this well-
meant offer. Without warning, he fairly took the kid's
breath away. He thrust the long-spouted oil can at
Luther with the injunction: "Here. Take this and
see if you know how to grease the old kettle's joints
without overlooking any of them."

That was a red-letter day for Luther.

The sometime expressed and long-cherished hope of
her firstborn becoming a prominent business man, or
perhaps a member of one of the learned professions,
faded further and further into the background for poor

Site of the Jones home at Cayce, Ky. Years later when the owner of this property conveyed it he stipulated that this grove of locust trees should not be disturbed but preserved in memory of Casey.

Ann Jones. At a loss for words to express that which overflowed her heart, she contemplated him wistfully.

Certainly at that time the keenest observer would have had difficulty detecting anything even remotely suggestive of the clerical or professional in Luther's speech or bearing. Not that he consciously bragged or aped the blistering blasphemies of the trainmen, but at that stage of his career he could not forego an occasional superior strut or refrain entirely from a certain vigorous style of language that often shocked his parents into a state of dumb agony.

But what definitely put an end to Luther's academic schooling was an urge to go to work in earnest, first on the farm of Eli P. Reeves, and later on the farm of Deacon Walls, both staunch pillars of the community. From what is known of Frank Jones, it is not unlikely that he encouraged the resolve, if he did not actually put the idea into his son's head in the first place. The pedagogue's robust family of children were outgrowing his modest stipend.

Luther's pay was small enough, but he had his "keep" in addition, and living was amazingly cheap in those days. Indeed, after contributing his share to the family budget, he started and maintained a savings account— the first sign of an instinctive thrift that grew to be habitual.

These changes in the family's condition had a direct bearing on the boy's future. Luther's contributions to the family exchequer, by becoming an established custom, were to affect one of the most critical intervals of his life; and the circumstances of his employment with Deacon Walls undoubtedly constituted the controlling factor in identifying him permanently with the railroad.

Like most boys, Luther was fond of those juvenile forms of baseball, known as "catball" and "townball," which were in high favor at the time. From these he had graduated to the national game proper, becoming an exceedingly proficient player, the mainstay and backbone of the Cayce *Dreadnaughts*. The old Deacon would be recognized today as a fan of the first magnitude and a fiery rooter for the home team. This was fortunate for Luther; for his duties on the farm were never allowed to interfere with his participation in the games of the *Dreadnaughts*. It was largely because he was a good baseball player that Luther obtained his first important connection with the railroad.

And now let us go with him on what turned out to be his last visit—as a callow stripling—to the Water Tank.

CHAPTER III

THE DECISION

IT HAD become a habit with Luther to be at the Water Tank when No. 22 pulled in. There were many other trains that stopped there, of course, but No. 22 arrived at the most convenient hour. Although he was now on a familiar footing with most of the train crews, who were accustomed to seeing the gawky, inquisitive boy with his inappeasable thirst for information, it was Bill Flickenger and Steve Gowdy whom he had found to be most amiable and willing to explain the things a boy wanted to know; even if Steve did rib him unmercifully.

There was one engineer who—unless he was laid out at Cayce by a meet order or to let a passenger train pass—drove slam-bang past as if there were no Water Tank at Cayce. Luther often gazed speculatively after his clattering drag as it vanished in the distance. He mentioned it one day to Bill and Steve.

"Does he carry enough water to last him to the terminal?"

"Does look that way," Bill Flickenger replied.

Steve was more explicit.

"If you ever start railroading as fireboy for Bose Lashley, you'll learn two things right off, Spigots.

23

They ain't a better engineer anywhere. And you'll have to work like hell bailing black diamonds. He don't spend much time setting on sidings."

"But it takes water to make steam," Luther insisted.

"Sure," said Steve. "But old Bose has his supply gauged to a drop. He knows just how many tanks he can run before he has to stop for water."

Luther got the impression that Lashley was a seamed and seasoned veteran of the throttle.

Bill Flickenger was usually on the right side of the cab of No. 22's locomotive, Steve was generally the fireman. Sometimes it would be somebody else. For occasionally Steve would be laid up with a mysterious malady which Bill Flickenger called a *katzenjammer* — an impressive sounding diagnosis that excited Luther's sympathetic concern. Steve was touchy about it, however, and the one time Luther anxiously inquired as to his sufferings while in its throes, he was gruffly invited to "Go to hell."

This particular morning, Steve's place was filled by a negro fireboy, one who didn't have the cheek to "let" the white boy clean his fire. Luther had reached the point where he no longer waited to be handed the tallowpot but simply possessed himself of it as a matter of course and set about oiling the rod cups while he and the engineer carried on a desultory conversation. The customary routine was followed this morning.

"No. 2 on time?" Luther asked, merely to make talk, for he already knew the train was running on time. He wouldn't have thought of showing up at the Water Tank without first stopping by the little "dee-po" telegraph office and informing himself respecting the movements of all trains.

And this morning, for the first time, it occurred to him that the fast running *Mr. Lashley* would not be waiting here for No. 2 to pass, with the terminal at Columbus only fourteen miles away. The reflection occasioned in him some vague but disturbing doubts, which, in loyalty to Bill Flickenger, he tried to brush away and forget.

Bill Flickenger did not bother to reply to his question. He said instead: "How come you're not busy with your farm chores? Holiday?"

"Baseball," was the succinct explanation. "My boss man is loony about baseball. We play the Jordan *Nonpareils* this evening; I got to ketch for the home team."

"He must be like our division superintendent," opined old Bill. "He'd ride the length of the division to see a ball game. . . . How tall are you, son?"

Luther had been uncomfortably aware that his tall, skinny frame was being subjected to a deliberate, calculating scrutiny by the engineer. Pointed reference to his overgrown size or tender years made him more awkward than ever.

" 'Round six foot, I reckon," he confessed, flushing.

"Add two-three inches to that," said old Bill judicially. "You're going to be a whale of a big man when you stop growing and fill out."

The engineer, in the Water Tank's shade, leaned comfortably against one of its heavy upholding timbers. One of the many never-ceasing drips from the immense tank barely missed him. He concluded:

"Must be nigh on to twenty-one, ain't you?"

Bill Flickenger's shrewd regard turned from the embarrassed stripling, and he craned round to appraise what Cayce had to offer—or as much of it as he could see.

Not much. Not one beautiful or inviting object within the field of vision. Not a thing that Engineer Bill Flickenger would have given two bits for. It was a frankly disparaging survey. Then his regard turned to rest once more upon Luther.

"Boy," Bill Flickenger solemnly enjoined, "get yourself out of this God-forsaken hole. If you aim ever to start knocking on a firebox door or flipping the rear end of a train, it's time you got going."

Luther lacked the temerity to confess that he was only turned fifteen, for it had been a trifle overpowering to be accepted on a status of maturity by a being as wise and exalted as Bill Flickenger. He was all at once a Man, ready to take his place among Men. Railroad Men.

It was opportune that No. 2 should come crashing and clattering by at this moment. The deafening uproar and the dust and debris-laden hurricane it kicked up were somehow in harmony with the boy's sudden feeling of uplift. He was only in a measure conscious of

No. 22's preparations for resuming its northward journey, yet every detail registered with him automatically.

Bill Flickenger swung up into his cab. The colored fireboy scrambled down the tender's coal pile to lend a hand in pushing the Johnson-bar into forward position and, next, fall to spreading coal over the fire. The injector vibrated with a deep rumbling violence that beat cruelly upon the eardrums. The conductor waved the highball, and from the whistle burst two short, sharp blasts—the signal to "release brakes." A tremendous exhaust from the huge funnel-shaped stack belched a volcano of cinders and black smoke skyward. Luther, oblivious to the hot cinders showering about him, thrilled to the prodigious banging and clattering that jolted the string of cars while the slack was being taken up.

Another moment and No. 22 was proceeding on its way northward.

When the Cayce *Dreadnaughts* met their perennial rivals, the Jordan *Nonpareils*, that afternoon, it may be safely assumed that they had to get along without the aid of Luther Jones. Furthermore, Deacon Walls was obliged to hire another farmhand.

For all the longings and urgings that had been budding in the boy's bosom burst into full flower. He was going to be a railroad engineer!

But it was not easy to set out at once upon the path best calculated to lead eventually to the righthand side of a locomotive cab.

First of all, and certainly the most serious obstacle, was his mother's inflexible opposition to any such ambition. Of the railroad and all its ramifications she harbored a holy dread. And Luther's love of his mother constituted one of his outstanding characteristics to the very end. He respected her wishes, and it was impossible for him to deny her authority so far as to be stubbornly disobedient. The habit of obedience had become ingrained. He had his work cut out for him. It took skillful argument to win from her even a begrudging consent, which was, in reality, scarcely more than a compromise. To get her to so much as listen to him he had to overcome an unyielding reluctance. But when the sun set that day, it set also upon her fondest plans for her firstborn.

Ann Nolen Jones was convinced that her boy had his heart set upon becoming an engineer and that no power on earth could budge him from that resolve. For her to refuse to temporize might mean complete estrangement; might drive the fledgling from its nest. Thus it came about that she was persuaded to attempt a compromise and meet him halfway. He might outgrow what she half-heartedly hoped was no more than a boyish whimsy.

It was agreed between them, accordingly, that he was to enter the commercial and not the mechanical side of railroading, and to that end he set out next day for Columbus, Kentucky, which at that time was the northern terminal of the Mobile & Ohio Railway, his purpose being to learn telegraphy in the company's offices.

An entry that Ann Jones made in the journal at this time is of extraordinary interest. In trying to win his mother's consent, Luther made much of a contrivance that Bill Flickenger had mentioned to him. Quoting what she set down: "A man named Westinghouse is said to have created a miracle—a brake for trains that operates by air! How absurd. Luther declares that they will be generally adopted by the railroads and that riding on the train will be as safe as attending church."

Strange that this revolutionizing safety device should become the indirect cause of more than one death in her family.

CHAPTER IV

QUEST FOR A JOB

ONLY fourteen miles separated Cayce from Columbus. The accommodation train—Irish Mail to the railroaders—was an institution of importance and did a flourishing business, both passenger and freight, taking care of all traffic that the through trains were obliged to pass by.

Luther was at that period of life commonly referred to in the vernacular as "half-baked," and was subject to a painful shyness when quizzed by his elders, especially those in positions of authority. There was a time when the baiting of men like Steve Gowdy made him squirm in an agony of mortification; but he had discovered that the more he overcame what was to him an appalling weakness, the less the men were disposed to make sport of him. His last ounce of will power often was called upon to muster a bold front, and when he succeeded the effect was one of exaggeration, flaunting a brazen insolence that he did not intend at all.

No, he did not mean to be brash or impudent; he meant only to stand his ground. His encounters with men like Steve had taught him a thing or two. If a fellow was ever to get anywhere he could not afford to let the "Steves" of this world impose upon him.

Accordingly, the next morning after his eventful talk with his mother, he was all ready to set forth. A sheaf of currency—exactly $100—was pinned securely in the inside pocket of his coat, shoddy and threadbare, but his best. All his other worldly possessions were stowed in an immense battered and cracked patent-leather valise, where they had ample room to roll and tumble around. The money was partly his own savings, the rest a fund which his mother had miraculously managed to lay by. The shabby valise concealed such of his personal effects as were not entirely worn out.

To his utter dismay, his heart was in his throat. No amount of hard swallowing could induce it to go back where it belonged. He was in the throes of an emotion that threatened to upset his plans and defeat his determination. A crushing realization of his greenness and unpreparedness overwhelmed him.

And the rest of the family—except his mother—were not helping the situation.

"My son," the dignified pedagogue enjoined, "be wary of strangers when they approach you."

"Gosh, yes!" Eugene put in. "Don't let anybody steal our valise."

"And always remember," his father pursued, "you are a gentleman."

Even Frank bethought him of an axiom, one of his father's favorites, which he had heard perhaps oftener than any other, and which was written, with elaborate Spencerian flourishes, across the top of the schoolroom blackboard. He now reminded his brother with smug complacency:

"Industry—Sobriety—Thrift—spell Success."

"Shut up!" the harassed boy yelled. "Give a fella a chance to think, won't you?"

He *was* thinking—thinking hotly that if he wasn't on the point of leaving he'd lick the stuffin' out of them crazy jackasses, Eugene and Frank.

But his mother took charge, as usual, and temporarily silenced the others. This was no time to be bombarding Luther with warnings and advice. She had admonished him fully already, and quite enough had been said by all. Now her chief concern was to see that he take with him every available thing necessary for his physical comfort.

All at once Luther's chin was up. He swaggered and assumed a contempt for their fears that he was far from feeling.

"Gosh! You all make me sick. You'd think I was headed for China 'stead of just up to Columbus."

"But you ain't ever even rode on the steam cars," Eugene truthfully persisted.

Luther glowered black resentment at his brother.

"You *would* say that. Listen, smart Alec. One of these days you'll see me running my own engine. If you don't take your hat off to me, I'll slap it off." He swallowed hard again and clutched the handle of the big valise. "I got to be off."

But his emotions continued to detain him. He stood

hesitantly on the threshold, looking nervously at one and then the other with ill-concealed affection, held by the spell of that tremendous moment: a tall, ungainly country jake in a cheap, worn suit that was much too small for his skinny frame, with unruly black hair sprouting from beneath a tight-fitting cloth cap of nondescript color. He was all eagerness to be off, yet, paradoxically, loath to depart; and filled with uncertainty and anxiety, frightful anxiety. So, to show his indifference to the warnings and lamentations of the family, he commenced whistling; an assumed note of unconcern that was decidedly off key.

Emma, who had been standing back, silent and tearful, now rushed impulsively at her oldest brother and threw her arms around him, hugging him tightly.

"Luther!" she whispered with quivering intensity. "Stay away from that awful river! Please!"

He stared down into her tragically earnest face, too startled to speak for a moment. Then he uttered stupidly: "Gosh, Sis! I thought you were going to jab a pin in me or pinch me—or somethin'."

She gave him an impatient shake.

"Kiss me good-by," she begged.

She stood up on tiptoe, and he stooped down and kissed her good-by.

It was not so surprising, on the other hand, that Eugene and Frank should, at the last moment, express a determination to accompany Luther as far as the "dee-po." But the boys had reckoned without knowledge of

his plans. He had no intention of breaking into his cap-
ital to part with the few cents necessary for train fare to
Columbus. Of course, the trainmen might refuse to let
him ride free, might even jeer at his presumption, but
these two little pests were not going to witness his dis-
comfort.

So, once they were safely out of sight and earshot of
the house, he halted and dropped the valise to the road-
way dust. He seized each of them with a determined
grasp upon the shirt collar, taking them completely by
surprise. The behavior of his two brothers, up to this
point, had been that of secretly anticipating something
dreadful to happen to him, and of being resolved not to
miss seeing it for anything in the world. Between
clenched teeth, he growled:

"Listen, you two. Scamper back home. Before I
rip the hides offen you."

Frank began to whimper. Eugene, at first, was disposed to bridle and resist such summary treatment.
Luther was gently but firmly rocking them back and
forth, and now he suddenly banged their heads together.

"Git!"

So fierce was his mien that, when he pushed them
away, they broke into a run without further ado.

It was Steve who first espied him. Steve had just
finished pulling the big spout back to upright position,
after filling the locomotive's tender tank. The manhole
lid was replaced, and he started to scramble down the
coal heap when his eye was caught by the sunlight flash-

ing from the monstrous old patent-leather valise. Steve had to stare hard before he could recognize the long-legged, unfamiliar figure approaching from the village with tremendous strides.

Then he pretended to be overwhelmed, as if by some stupendous apparition. His jaw dropped, his eyes bulged, his prominent Adam's apple jerked spasmodically up and down. The top of a tender tank is no place to indulge in acrobatics, but Steve gave a fine performance of staggering backward, while his hands groped in mid-air, seeking a sustaining hold that was not there, to keep himself from toppling overboard. He made it unmistakable that he was completely flabbergasted. Words burst from him in a tone of exaggerated amazement.

"Bill! My God! Lookit! Do you see what I see?"

Startled from his never-ending job of oiling the rod cups while his engine was at rest, Bill Flickenger glanced round to take in Luther's bizarre appearance. He too stared.

Steve demanded: "Am I seein' things again? Or is that Spigots?"

The engineer was not long in comprehending the situation. Only yesterday he had urged the lad to cut loose from his sterile environment.

"So," said Flickenger, while Steve clambered down the coal to the gangway and thence to the right of way. "You ain't wasting any time, Bud. Columbus bound?"

Luther nodded and cleared his throat. His voice

lately had acquired a disconcerting trick of breaking unexpectedly into a ludicrous falsetto squeak, and he wanted it to sound hoarse and manly, like Steve's. He was ignorant, then, of the vast quantities of alcohol that had to be consumed over a long period of time to produce that particular degree and quality of hoarseness.

"I'm going to get me——" he tried to proclaim, but that daggone voice! Treacherously it betrayed him. He began again: "I'm going to get me a job on this man's railroad."

In the long looks exchanged between the engineer and fireman, doubt and uncertainty over the first step they were expected to take were intermingled. Finally light broke over Steve's red, elongated face.

"By golly, Bill! Have you forgot?"

Bill evidently had. "Sure enough," he confessed, suddenly remembering. "The Major's at Columbus, ain't he? If he don't pull out before we get there." Then to Luther:

"Do your folks know about this?"

The boy nodded, afraid to speak unless necessary.

"All right with them, hey? Well, I reckon we can arrange it with Mr. Galloway to haul you to Columbus in the dog house."

Mr. Galloway—who would have wondered at the formal address inasmuch as he was commonly known as Spud—happened to be No. 22's conductor; "dog house" was railroadese for caboose.

But Steve thwarted this plan.

"Like hell!" he yelled. "Spigots will ride with us. It's only fourteen miles to Columbus."

He had seized the battered old valise, whose size indicated that some effort would be required to lift it, and when it shot up with unexpected ease, he became abruptly motionless, holding the shiny object aloft. A queer expression overspread his face. His voice dropped to an unexpected gentleness.

"Fella, what you aimin' to fill this thing with?"

Somehow this sudden honest solicitude banished Luther's last apprehension. He grinned broadly at the fireman.

"Beans," he said. "Beans for your old mudhen."

"There's the highball," announced Flickenger. "Get aboard. Guess we can take a chance on getting fired for hauling the kid that short distance."

"Huh," Steve grunted. "You know what? Spigots'll show us two apple knockers how a engine ought to be run."

CHAPTER V

"CASEY" JONES

THIS was Luther Jones' very first ride on a railroad
train. As familiar as he had become with trains, especially locomotives, it was truly strange that never before had he known the experience of being on a moving
train. Even more extraordinary, however, was the
fact that his first ride should have been in the locomotive's cab—right in there with the engineer and fireman, and at their invitation. Nothing could have
seemed more remote and unattainable than this the
object of his fondest dream, and here, with breath-
taking suddenness, in the twinkling of an eye, it had
come true.

Little can be told about that ride, because he remained more or less in a daze. The occasion undoubtedly was one of purely delirious, enchanting bliss. Details registered in his subconsciousness, of course. Night
after night, for many months, dream flashes came to
him: of Bill Flickenger's hand upon the throttle, of
Bill tugging at the whistle cord, of Bill peering at the
steam and water gauges; of Steve sliding from his
leather cushion to bang open the firebox door and shovel
coal, of Steve making a great show of pulling the bell
cord; of a lurching and bumping and jerking this way

38

and that and a constant shaking up that left him sore for
days. The old 5-foot broad-gauge mudhens were not
noted for their riding qualities, and construction had a
long way to go from the light rails and bumpy roadbeds of that day to the heavy steel and smooth, rock-
ballast of the present.

Luther was left standing upon the cinders in the
Columbus Mobile & Ohio Railway yards. Some moments were required for him to recover his breath and
collect his stampeded wits. No. 22's locomotive had
been cut loose from her drag and was rolling away
toward the roundhouse, between long lines of side-
tracked cars.

Otherwise his surroundings registered only in a mechanical sort of fashion: rows of cars, box cars and
flats, strung along some of the side-tracks, and a locomotive, with a light feather of steam gently sputtering
from her pop-valve, waiting at one end of a string of
freight cars for orders to go somewhere. He caught
an unmistakable smell of the river. Above a conglom-
erate collection of levee shacks, a pair of towering stacks
and the wheel-house of a steamboat could be seen, all
within a short stone's throw. Only a few men were
visible at the time, however, and the yards were cor-
respondingly quiet. Nobody paid any attention to the
forlorn figure with the shiny patent-leather valise.

Two things penetrated to his active comprehension
simultaneously. He was hanging on to the valise with
a vise-like grip, and Steve was shouting something back

at him, before the engine was hid from view—something which Steve evidently had been trying to impress upon him for some minutes.

"Talk up to 'em, kid. Don't be scared. Tell the Major you're a baseball player. Good luck, Spigots!"

That was the last time anybody ever called him Spigots. And he never again saw Steve Gowdy alive.

A sharp clicking of telegraph instruments drew his attention at last to a long, low wooden building which housed the railway offices and freight house. It was only a matter of seconds to enter and find his way to a room, where the clatter of sounders and relays suddenly hammered upon his ears, and where a half-dozen or so men were gathered. Most of them were busy about something; two or three apparently had nothing more arduous to occupy them than to stay motionless on the most comfortable seats they had been able to find, ranging from a nail keg to the top of a table.

Inside the door, he let the valise drop to the floor and struck an attitude which he hoped would disguise his trembling frame and distract notice from his pounding heart. He stood as erectly as he knew how, with left hand resting upon hip and arm jauntily akimbo, his head tilted backward in order to peer below the visor of his cap. Because he was a stranger, conversation ceased, and all eyes turned curiously to survey him.

He noisily cleared his throat. Voice, don't do me wrong now! How earnestly he hoped it would sound hoarse and manly, like Steve's!

"Who's the boss here?" he inquired.

Despite his cocksure bearing, the long-legged lad in misfit clothes, and badly in need of a haircut, did not present an impressive appearance. Nevertheless he held the attention of everybody there for a long moment.

At last, a gray, depressed-looking little man, who sat at a broad, dingy and much-battered desk thumbing a mountainous stack of waybills, ventured to speak. His tone and manner were without enthusiasm.

"If you want to pay me money, I am. If it's trouble you're looking for, talk to some of these other gents. What you want?"

"I've come to go to work," was the blunt reply. "That may not mean money to you, mister, but I know durn well it won't cause you trouble."

A laugh rippled round the company. The little man, with sharpened interest, asked: "Who sent you here?"

Luther's spirits took a dive. He was obliged to confess: "Nobody. I just come."

Fortunately for the boy one of the company spoke up.

"Bud, ain't you the boy who's been hanging round the Water Tank at Cayce for some time?"

Luther's attention was thus directed to a slim young fellow, garbed in the high-bibbed overall and black cap outfit which he long ago had come to associate with engineers and firemen as their identifying uniform. This young man half-sat on a corner of a desk, a foot

on the floor and one long leg bracing himself, a hooked
knee caught in his clasped hands. A pair of keen gray
eyes belied his drawling speech. A fireman, Luther
concluded.

The boy nodded. His arm was no longer jauntily
akimbo, his head no longer confidently reared. He
amplified:

"Off an' on—I guess it's been all of two years."

The interrogator's interest quickened perceptibly.

"So," he said thoughtfully, "you've graduated from
the Cayce Water Tank. What next?"

The room was so arranged that a recess at one end
extended back perhaps a dozen feet, with a door on
each side and a door at the end. The end door opened
at this juncture and a man unobtrusively entered. He
was behind the others but almost directly in front of
Luther, who absently noted him standing more or less
in shadow. The man's attention was immediately fo-
cused upon the boy, and he stopped to listen.

The young fellow on the table corner repeated his
question: "What next, Bud? You going to be a railroader?"

Again the boy nodded, rather dismally now. But
he remembered his resolve and plucked desperately at
his sinking spirits, trying to ignore the amusement in
the battery of eyes turned upon him. He hoped his
voice wouldn't crack. "I'm going to be an engineer,"
he stoutly replied. Then, with diminished fervor:
"But I got to learn telegraphy first."

"Do tell!" another, whom Luther recognized as a trainman acquaintance, abruptly spoke up. "I know this kid. He's catcher for the Cayce baseball nine. Send for Buck Ewing, somebody. And he wants to be an engineer. Good God'll mighty!"

"Close your trap," Luther's questioner commanded, without turning his head. "If he wants to be an engineer hard enough, he will be. Having to learn telegraphy first, though—I don't get that."

Telegraphy was not the customary route to the right-hand side of a locomotive cab; not a regulation qualification for an eagle-eye.

The man in the recess created a diversion by coming on into the big room. Luther now perceived that his carriage was soldierly; a man in his early fifties, with iron-gray hair and sideburns, with shrewd but kindly regard. He at once commanded the attention of the others present.

He said to Luther: "I've seen you play baseball, son. Last Fourth of July, the Cayce *Dreadnaughts* played the Columbus *Hornets*, didn't they?"

Luther murmured respectfully: "I reckon they did, sir." This man must be one of the "brass hats" he had heard Bill Flickenger and Steve Gowdy talk about.

The other pursued: "It was the ninth inning. The score was seven to five, favor of the *Hornets*." This was less a statement than a question, so Luther confirmed it.

"Yes, sir."

"The *Dreadnaughts* were at bat with two men out, when a boy about your size and build stepped up to the plate. Cayce had runners on first and second. This young fellow slammed the first pitched ball so hard it never was found, and Cayce beat the *Hornets* eight to seven. You are the boy that cracked that home run. Your names is Jones, isn't it?"

"Yes, sir."

The newcomer advanced to where the young fellow was seated on the table edge. The latter acknowledged his approach by dropping the elevated foot to the floor and assuming a more respectful attitude. The two engaged in a low-pitched conversation, of which Luther had the uncomfortable feeling that he was the subject. Their eyes frequently rested upon him, and now and then he heard Bill Flickenger's name mentioned. The entire company waited silently until the pair were finished. Finally the young man said: "I believe it would be the thing to do, Major."

The young man swung round to face Luther again.

"What did you say your name is, Bud?"

"Jones," Luther told him.

"Jones," the young fellow repeated, making a wry face, as if the name had a bad taste. "Another Jones. There's Dave and Mort and Spider and Winkler Jones, not to mention Hub and Fred Jones. Have I overlooked any of 'em, Major?"

The Major's gray eyes twinkled. "Stewart Jones," he supplied.

Arrival at Columbus

"By Stewart," the young fellow pursued, "I take it you mean Stew Jones." He counted rapidly on his fingers. "Seven Joneses on the company's payroll, all working on this division. What a mess of Joneses!" Then once more to Luther: "What's the rest of your name?"

"John Luther," the shamefaced boy owned up.

The young man appeared to be startled.

"What?" he roared. "John Luther Jones? A hell of a name for a railroad engineer." He stared fixedly at Luther. "You belong to Cayce, Bud. Cayce. That's what it's got to be—Cayce. It will distinguish you from the common herd of Joneses. Cayce Jones is a proper monicker for an engineer, too." His regard swept over the company. He ended:

"Hear that, you tramps? This is CAYCE Jones."

Someone in the group spoke up:

"But, Bose, who, off the Jackson Division, ever heard of Cayce? It's only a flag-stop. Folks'll think he's Irish and that his name's spelt C-A-S-E-Y."

The young man slapped his thigh in an ecstacy of delight.

"So much the better!" exclaimed he. "The very thing! Good old Irish name of Casey. Casey Jones. What a lulu of a name for an engineer! Casey Jones!"

The Major laughed. So did the others.

But of this and the young man's concluding words Luther was scarcely aware. That name . . . Bose . . . had arrested his attention. Could this young fellow—he didn't look much older than Luther, though his voice didn't seem disposed to break with embarrassing consequences—could he be the famous Bose Lashley? *   The engineer who had a reputation for running by water tanks?   Who always ran slam-bang past the one at Cayce?   The boy now recognized a certain deference in the bearing of the others toward the one called Bose which convinced him that this was really the man.   He was thrilled from his toes to the roots of his hair.

He became aware that the Major was speaking, addressing him by that outlandish nickname—Casey.

"S-s-s-sir?" he stammered.

"I was asking you, Casey Jones, how you would like to play ball with the *Hornets.*"

The full significance of the Major's proposal suddenly flashed into Luther's bewildered consciousness. He was rendered speechless with joy and the Major, reading the unmistakable answer in the boy's radiant countenance, smilingly turned to the depressed little man at the big flat desk.

"Miller," he said, and when Miller looked up, "make a place for this young man.   He wants to become a telegraph operator."   And to Luther: "When Miller gets through with you, find Buck Ewing.   Tell him I sent you.   I am Major Hosford.†   He will be glad to have a player like you."

* See Appendix, note 10.
† See Appendix, note 9.

CHAPTER VI

CUB OPERATOR

CASEY JONES had many reasons for knowing Buck Ewing, variously hostler at the M. & O. roundhouse, straw boss with a work crew, switchman, and sometimes both engineer and fireman of the Columbus yard dinghy, as the M. & O. switch-engine was known; but chiefly he was recalled by Casey as captain of the *Hornets*—a tough individual who usually had to be ganged up on to settle a close or disputed decision. But just now Casey had more serious things in mind.

The succeeding three or four days were sufficient for the youth to begin to get his bearings and to adjust himself to his new environment: mental processes that brought certain disillusionments and toughening experiences, but without in any degree abating his determination to become an engineer.

To learn that no stipend was connected with his apprenticeship was disheartening; nor could he hope for any until he had attained to the rating of, at least, "ham" operator. A "ham," he was informed, was an operator who was able to undertake only the simplest telegraphing jobs, such as were to be found in the smallest, least important whistle-post offices, where about all the operator had to do was revel in silent loneliness and OS (report by) the trains that whizzed past the office windows. What a depressing prospect for one who aspired to be a famous engineer!

His $100, he sharply realized, would have to be spread over the period of his schooling. The day operator in the Columbus offices, Cunningham—better known as Cunny—had told him that, by diligent application, he might qualify as a "ham" by the expiration of eight months. The boy inwardly groaned. Those eight months stretched far away into a remote future like so many epochs.

Cunny had amplified: "OS-ing trains is mere routine—when all trains are on time. But schedules sometimes go cockeyed. So you got to know how to take and repeat back a train order, and how to handle railway messages. You'll have to handle whatever freight and express there might be on the night trick, too, and take care of the billing. All that will come to you, though, while you're learning to pound the key—if," he gloomily ended, "you ever do learn."

Panic fluttered in the neophyte's bosom.

"Gosh!" he cried, "you think I'm that stupid?"

Cunny subjected the gangling lad to a critical survey. He replied judicially:

"Well, you never can tell. Some fellas take to telegraphing like a duck takes to water. On the other hand there are fellas who just naturally aren't built right ever to learn. In between they come in varying degrees of stupidity; one fella gets to be a pretty good brass-

pounder in two-three months, maybe, while the next
one plugs along for two-three years before qualifying
for a diploma. It all depends on which class you're in,
Horatio."

Thus was it put squarely up to him. His becoming
a telegraph operator—assuming that he had the aptitude to learn—depended entirely upon his application
to the job.

Not being a regular employee was, however, offset
by a number of compensating factors. His time was
very much his own. Except when his services were required he was largely his own boss—which meant much
in a day when the work period or "trick" was of twelve
hours' duration, from seven to seven o'clock.

He was sensible enough to realize that only by industry and willingness to lend a helping hand could
he expect to win the friendship of the men in the office
and freight house and retain the standing he had so
luckily acquired here. It was no place for idlers when
there was work to be done.

In this respect, the number of men employed directly and indirectly in the railroad's business was a
revelation to the boy from the backwoods. An army
of workers was necessary because virtually all freight
had to be transferred between two connecting railroads,
and also between the M. & O. and its fleet of river
boats.

The yards were conveniently located some two miles

south of the little town, in contact with the loading wharves on the Mississippi River. All southbound Mobile & Ohio trains originated at Columbus, and therefore the southbound flow of traffic was largely regulated by the volume received from feeder sources. Also a growing commerce flowed northward over the Mobile & Ohio which had to be taken care of at Columbus, either over the connecting railway or via steamboat to the Illinois Central at Cairo, Illinois—some twenty-four miles.

Like conditions cannot be found today at any inland terminal or junction, and when the Mobile & Ohio adopted standard-gauge track and, in 1886, completed its trunkline to Cairo and thence to St. Louis, Columbus became but a memory as a railroad center and all but faded from the map.

But this state of affairs and all that it signified was much too big to be taken in by the boy all at once, and as his knowledge and understanding broadened, conditions were accepted by him as regular and commonplace—as indeed they were at the time. When cars were jacked up and 5-foot wheel trucks were replaced by standard-gauge trucks, or *vice versa*, in order that trainloads of freight might proceed on their way, north or south, he looked upon the operation as a marvel of progressiveness and up-to-date enterprise. That such methods were cumbrous, tedious and costly was fully realized by the controlling spirits of the railroad, however, who suffered many a headache trying to devise and put into operation ways and means of improving upon them.

Casey was immediately concerned only by the circumstances that directly affected himself. He might absent himself from the offices whenever he wanted to, of course; nobody would try to stop him, nor did anyone have authority to do so. Yet if he showed lack of interest in the work or indulged an inclination to loaf, he knew that his continued presence would not be tolerated. But the office personnel were unanimously enthusiastic in approving his absence whenever the *Hornets* needed him. When a game was to be played he was given to understand in no uncertain terms that his place was on the diamond with his teammates, rather than bending over a telegraph sounder trying to capture the dots and dashes being clicked off.

So it may be seen that his conference with Buck Ewing had been in every way satisfactory. Buck was manager of the *Hornets* as well as the team's catcher. He was in need of a good first-baseman. He had cause for knowing how well the Cayce stripling could play ball and, what was more to the point, what an eye he had for hitting the ball when hits counted most. So the erstwhile *Dreadnaughts'* catcher was made regular first-baseman of the *Hornets*, in which position he acquitted himself with conspicuous credit during succeeding months.

Trainmen and other "rails" came and went constantly through the offices. Those who did not know Casey at all, or only slightly, were disposed to pass him by with no more than a detached, incurious glance until Lem Miller, the agent, or Cunny would call out: "What's the hurry, Pete? Stop long enough to shake hands with Casey Jones. He's our new first-baseman. Buck has just taken him on. Casey's a wizard with the bat, Buck says."

Quickly Pete's attitude would change to one of effusive cordiality! Being a student operator wasn't worth mentioning, it seemed. Therefore the boy discreetly held his tongue, letting the information come out from one of the others, merely as an unimportant detail.

The best part of all this, from his point of view, was that he could expect to be paid a dollar or so—sometimes as much as three dollars—whenever the *Hornets* went against a team in their class and the gate receipts warranted. To earn that much money by playing baseball was something to write home and tell the folks about. Miller and Cunny informed him that, work permitting, virtually all of the railroad employees, including the levee hands, turned out to root for the *Hornets*. Frequently they deadheaded in from distant points along the M. & O. division, and the division superintendent, Major E. S. Hosford, and others of the brass hats were often spectators. The *Hornets*, the boy soon perceived, were sponsored more by the railroad than by the community at large.

Time taken from the office to play baseball or indulge in other daytime activities could not be counted as lost, for he could make up for it by putting in as many hours at night as he desired. Charley Spencer, the night operator, was a glum individual to associate with, betraying interest in nothing that Casey could discover—not even in the *Hornets*, nor in a student operator who would have liked to talk about becoming a famous engineer some day. The apprentice, consequently, was left much to his own devices during the night shift. As soon as he mastered the mechanics of the Morse code, he could occupy himself to his heart's content with the dummy set of instruments with which most telegraph offices were equipped.

Conductors and engineers of all M. & O. trains, both arrivals and departures, were required to register at the Columbus office—departing trains to get their clearances and running orders. Orders were telegraphed from the division dispatchers' office at Jackson, Tennessee. In this way, the student renewed the acquaintances he had formed at the Water Tank and made many new ones: the conductors and engineers and flagmen of the passenger trains, and men like Bose Lashley, who customarily ran the Cayce water tank. Bill Flickenger, of course. But not Steve Gowdy. He secretly wished that Steve would drop in to see him.

Flickenger and Lashley relieved his feeling of strangeness and loneliness by displaying a friendliness that warmed his heart. *They* knew that some day he would be an engineer, even if his changing voice did treat him shabbily when he wanted to be most impressive.

On Casey's second day at Columbus, Bose Lashley came in with his conductor for their clearance and running orders. They were in charge of an extra-south.

"Well," the young engineman greeted him across the train register, "how's old No. 31 feeling today?"

At the boy's blank look Lashley simulated extreme astonishment.

"What! You don't know what a 31 is? I expected you'd be ready to start dispatching trains by this time. You might as well learn now as later. Thirty-one, my boy, is code for a train order for two or more trains to meet and pass each other somewhere else besides on the main line."

The boy gasped: "Why, they couldn't do that!"

To which the engineer drily returned: "They've been known to try."

The first time Bill Flickenger came in to register with his conductor, Spud Galloway, Casey ventured to inquire about Steve Gowdy. Flickenger, pencil in hand, bent over the open register and shook his head with an air of solemn melancholy.

"Bad," he said. "Durn bad."

"Katzenjammer?" asked Casey.

"Worst ever," said Bill Flickenger.

An hour or so later the boy received the first tragic shock of his life, one that gave him food for many moments of sober thought. Steve, he learned, was enraged by No. 21 pulling out without him. With jangled nerves and muscles twitching, he had come storming to the yards in a wild state of mind, determined to hop a southbound passenger train and overtake his drag. Ignoring protests of fellow workers, before any of them realized his intention, he attempted to swing aboard No. 1 as it swept past.

He was thrown beneath the wheels.

It happened within a stone's throw of the offices. There was excited commotion in the yards for some minutes. Fortunately for the lad's subsequent peace of mind, his rush to the scene was checked when he overheard what had befallen and who the victim was. The shock stunned him. He retreated to the telegraph room, white and shaken, and would not venture forth again until the mangled body had been removed and quiet restored.

When he went to his tiny room that night, he shoved the old patent-leather valise far under his bed, out of sight. He could not bear to look at it, seeing Steve holding it aloft and regarding him with sudden compassion. And when, at length, he blew out his light and crawled into bed, tears wet his pillow. More than once, before he fell asleep, he muttered into the darkness:

"Spigots!"

Next morning Steve Gowdy's body was shipped to his former home at Jackson for burial. The episode laid an emotional strain upon Casey, for, despite the man's hard, rough exterior, he had been a knowing and sympathetic friend. To the untried lad his going was a distinct loss, and nobody mourned for Steve with deeper feeling than did he.

The local weekly newspaper carried a full account of the accident together with a complimentary biographical sketch of the victim. This and the notice of the funeral arrangements gave Casey the idea of starting a scrap-book, to which he added from time to time for many years.

CHAPTER VII

RAILROAD BOULEVARD—WALLACE SAUNDERS

IT IS difficult to imagine the railroads of the Unite
States trying to move traffic, freight and passenger,
over three different widths of track. Bearing in mind
that the width of wheel trucks on all rolling-stock—
locomotives and cars—is fixed, not adjustable, the notion seems preposterous.

Nevertheless, at the time Luther Jones arrived in
the railroad yards at Columbus, such a condition prevailed; a condition which, if it were to be suddenly im-
posed upon the country's railroads today, would halt
trains everywhere, blockade the bulk of the nation's inland commerce, force passengers to resort to other
means of travel, and create havoc generally. The result would amount to a national calamity.

The condition may be very well illustrated by the
situation in this respect at Columbus, for it was much
the same at terminals and junction points the country
over, with the further aggravation that terminals and
traffic transfer points were, relatively, more numerous
and closer together then than now.

Mention has already been made of the Mobile &
Ohio's track width of five feet. This width was known

as broad-gauge. Then there were widths of track commonly in use known as narrow gauge. But there was rapidly coming into use still a third width of track that measured 4 feet 8½ inches, which before long was accepted as standard gauge, supplanting all other gauges used by the common carrier railways of all countries.

Columbus, prior to the early '80's, was an important junction for two primary reasons, namely: the Mobile & Ohio connected there by ferry with the St. Louis, Iron Mountain & Southern Railroad, and it also handled transfer traffic with the Illinois Central. Futhermore, Columbus was at that time the northern terminal of the Mobile & Ohio.

Shortly previous to 1878, the Iron Mountain road changed its gauge from 5 feet to the new 4 feet 8½ inch gauge, which permitted its entrance into the Union Depot at St. Louis, then the undisputed railroad center of the rapidly growing Middle West. However, the change that facilitated train movements at St. Louis had quite the opposite effect at the Columbus end of the line by causing a very real obstruction there. As a direct consequence of the change, transshipment of traffic between the two railroads could be made in only two ways, both of which were costly and resulted in delay of traffic movement.

First, traffic could be unloaded from the cars of one road and reloaded into the cars of the other. Or, second, the cars could be jacked up and the wheel trucks changed to fit the different gauge tracks. Facilities for this operation were available at Columbus, and actually were utilized in the through operation of trains!

With respect to the connection between the Mobile & Ohio and the Illinois Central, one more unwieldy method of handling traffic was encountered. Transfer was effected by means of river boats plying between Columbus and Cairo, and the great volume of freight thus handled is indicated by the number of steamboats built and put into service for this purpose.

Forerunner of the historical fleet of steamboats was the *Dan Abell*. Then followed the *Arlington, Gen. Anderson* and *Illinois*, three large side-wheelers which were expected to make the twenty-four mile run between Columbus and Cairo in an hour but never did except, possibly, in cut-off conditions during high water.

This fleet was supplemented by still another large steamboat, the *W. Butler Duncan*, built at Jeffersonville for the transfer between Columbus and East Cairo, and which continued in service until the Mobile & Ohio began using the Illinois Central bridge between Cairo and East Cairo.

It was not until 1884 that the Mobile & Ohio adopted standard gauge track. On July eighth of that year the change was made over the entire road between Columbus and Mobile, a distance of 472 miles, in one day!

Thereafter, of course, the road's rolling-stock could move between tidewater at Mobile and St. Louis over a track of uniform gauge. The date of Columbus's decline was marked by this change.

For several weeks following Steve Gowdy's tragic death, life at Columbus was uneventful for Casey. Then he was suddenly brought into contact with powerfully active forces—evil forces. Two revolver shots that shattered the calm of a quiet Sabbath, and the whine of a ricocheting bullet past his head, jarred him to a realization of the stark wickedness that flourished under his very nose.

Not that he had been entirely blind to what went on about him, but during the intervening days the process of storing up impressions of things never before seen or imagined was necessarily gradual.

For the most part, the extraordinary panorama unfolding before him was incomprehensible. The sordid show excited his liveliest curiosity, interspersed as it was by the roar and clatter and banging of passing trains that almost brushed the loading platforms and the operators' big bay window; the noisy shunting of cars in the yards, and the comings and goings of the men who worked about the place; the bellowing of river boats; the creaking of winches and the puffing fussiness of the donkey-engines operating them—in short, the medley of sounds of stir and bustle and activity generally that pervaded the place.

Instinctively clean-minded, the saloons and brothels that clustered like festering sores on the side of the

yards away from the river—as was the case at many railway terminals—aroused in his adolescent mind an unpleasant disturbing wonder. With them he hazily
associated certain familiar catch phrases of the backwoods
revivalists; *doorways to hell* . . . *gilded palaces of sin*
. . . *scarlet women* . . . *the woman with the attire of*
an harlot . . . *her house is the way to hell, going down*
to the chambers of death. But they did not convey a
definite meaning of anything in his experience. Now he
was hearing the men discuss things that made his flesh
crawl, while only dimly sensing what they were talking
and laughing about.

As for Lem Miller, the M. & O. agent, he avoided
any reference to what he called the "hell holes" and
"sinks of iniquity," over across the tracks, unless they
were forced upon his attention. It was apparent that
they engendered in his mild nature an extreme repug-
nance.

But Cunny and most of the other fellows liked to
joke and brag about the licentiousness and lewdness,
with which they were all more or less familiar, some of
the talk being so filthy that the boy moved out of earshot. Respecting Cunny, however, Casey began early
to suspect that the operator's knowing air and sly in-
sinuations were derived less from personal experiences
than from a desire to impress upon the callow student
that he was a very devil of a fellow. The inmates of
the brothels he called chippies, and the trainmen who
frequented the dives were chippy chasers.

Buck Ewing was more brutally frank. Expounding a sound philosophy, he declared: "A fella can't lay round them whores all the time and keep fit to play with the *Hornets*," then weakened the force of his logic by adding, with an avidity that made his lips quiver and his eyes moisten:

"You seen that slim little gal over at Gertie Blake's yet? The one called Garnet?"

Casey didn't know whether he had or not; he didn't know one of the girls from another. Buck Ewing waxed eloquent.

"Fella, she's a peach. I'll take you over to see her some time. Dark hair—dark eyes. Only seventeen. Pretty as a spotted pup. She's a money mint for that old bat, Gertie Blake."

Somehow mention of the girl's tender age stirred up a strong revulsion in Casey. The horrified way in which he stared at the captain of the *Hornets* was so open that Buck hastily shifted the conversation back to baseball.

From the big bay window where the telegraph instruments and switchboard were located, where the operator on duty spent most of the hours of his trick, three of the more notorious of the joints were plainly in the line of vision, whenever a passing train or one standing on the house track did not hide them.

First, directly opposite and most conspicuous, was a two-story red brick that stood where an unpaved street ended at the right of way. The ground floor was oc-

cupied by Red Donlin's saloon, the upper floor by Sadie
Carlisle and her girls.

Next to it, parallel to the right of way, was the dingy
one-story frame where Gertie Blake held forth, and
then came one known as the Peach Orchard, operated by
two personable women, Pearl and Puggy Lorraine, reputed to be sisters. A half-dozen or so shacks of lesser
popularity completed the row of bawdy houses.

No public thoroughfare paralleled the railway yards
at this point, but a narrow, unauthorized and unpaved
pathway facilitated access to the houses fronting on the
yards. The community's weekly newspaper had
facetiously dubbed this path "Railroad Boulevard,"
and, when occasion arose, the inmates of the houses
were referred to as "soiled doves." Hence, mention
in a news story of a "soiled dove of Railroad Boulevard" was accepted by the severely virtuous readers of
the period as an euphemism which, while clearly intel-
ligible to them, was not too flagrantly immodest to of-
fend sensitive souls, and which—so they fondly believed—conveyed no meaning whatever to the chaste
minds of innocent youths and young ladies.

A stairway inside the red brick connected a number
of private partitioned rooms, back of the barroom, with
the upstairs; a handy convenience. On the outside
front of the building was another stairway, uncovered
but with a handrail, that rose from the rear of Donlin's
to a railed platform or landing, likewise giving access
to Sadie Carlisle's domain but open to public view.

From this vantage point one could look down across a narrow, dirty alley-way, into the cluttered, weed-grown yard surrounding Gertie Blake's less pretentious frame structure. Now and again one or more of Sadie Carlisle's "doves" came out on the landing and chatted with the inmates of Gertie Blake's joint.

Underneath the wooden stairs was piled a welter of empty beer kegs, empty liquor bottles, broken boxes and crates, and many years' accumulation of trash. Innumerable monstrous gray rats found refuge here; almost any time of the day they might be detected slinking into the open or scurrying back to cover.

In such places, in the glare and glitter of the bar-rooms, and amid the hush and heady perfumes that curtained windows hid, the stream of life ran hotly, sometimes flaming into appalling bursts of savagery and tragedy. Nightly the lights glared; a reek compounded of unwholesome air, alcohol, cheap cosmetics and sweating human bodies assailed the nostrils; meaningless howls and silly laughter, shouted profanity and obscenities rang out above the roaring of maudlin ditties and the banging of tinny pianos by pasty-faced "professors" with needle-dotted arms.

Hell holes, sinks of iniquity, these spots were, unquestionably. But the unsophisticated lad, who sometimes stared across at them in wonder and awe, was to encounter in this putrescent atmosphere what grew to be one of the strangest relationships of his life, that with the little darky, Wallace Saunders. As he stared and wondered, one never could have guessed how his thoughts associated incongruous details, how they drew unexpected conclusions.

After his talk with Buck Ewing, for instance, he could not view any of the women without wondering how they had looked and acted when they were seventeen and younger. They were all innocent girls, once, like Emma. Even fat, coarse-featured Gertie Blake, who could shriek obscenities until one's ears curled. And the Lorraine sisters, who were still pretty and whose behavior in public was generally modest, could be as noisy as the loudest when they were drunk.

And the wizened little Negro man, black as coal, who served as janitor for Red Donlin and handy man for the dovecotes—he was an anomaly. His unflagging industry and nimble alertness were in sharp contrast with the lethargy that hung over the dives, daily, until late afternoon. Constantly, under his breath, he sang or hummed tunes characterized by the surprising intervals and queer minor cadences peculiar to his race. He seemed to be so detached from his surroundings, so alien to their atmosphere, so little a part of them, that one might picture him as serving a nunnery in like capacities with precisely the same demeanor. Casey never tired of watching the out-door activities of the little darky.

Late one afternoon he saw a woman come out and stand idly on the landing at Sadie Carlisle's. There was something in her bearing that at once arrested and held his attention. She was tall, her movements grace-

ful. One hand held her negligee tightly about her,
outlining a fine figure. She was not near enough for
him to distinguish her features clearly, but he had never
seen anything like the way the sun, nearly set, shone
upon her wealth of copper-colored hair.

He was disturbed by Cunny's tremblingly eager
whisper, almost at his ear:

"That's her! That's Sadie Carlisle! Isn't she a
corker?"

The boy no more than half heard. Only seventeen, he
was thinking; back in the past she had been a schoolgirl
—gay, laughing happily, unspoiled. . . . He turned
to Cunny.

"What?" he asked.

"She's the Madame," Cunny ran on. "Damn' particular, she is. She has a lover. Won't stand for any
foolishness in *her* joint. . . ."

By this time Casey himself was all atremble. He had
seen something that thrilled him with mingled emotions, something that fascinated him. For Sadie Carlisle
was doing the most *risque,* the most daring thing he had
ever heard of a woman doing.

She was smoking a cigarette, and with evident en-
joyment.

The dinghy, manned by Buck Ewing, puffed by on
the house track, shoving a half-dozen empty "high"
cars ahead of it. After it had passed, the woman was
no longer to be seen.

He found himself watching for her, half hoping to

see her repeat this upsetting yet strangely interesting performance. Even a male who smoked a cigarette those days was looked at askance. For a woman to do so was more than an impropriety; it unequivocally branded her for what she was. He loitered outside, along the office building, when he should have been busy with his Morse code; even out upon the yard tracks, dodging trains and shunted strings of cars, venturing thrillingly close to the red brick.

On one occasion the wizened darky, emerging suddenly from Donlin's saloon, came upon him there among the yard tracks. The black boy ducked his bullet head and grinned amiably at Casey, then hurried up the yards in the direction of the roundhouse, singing softly to himself. He carried a parcel under one arm, and Casey watched until he disappeared behind a string of freight cars on a siding. When the darky returned, Casey was still standing there. He spoke.

"Boy, you totin' whiskey to some of the men?"

The little negro grimaced and bowed and scraped obsequiously. It struck Casey that his face was exactly like a monkey's.

"No, suh, boss—not whiskey. Gin."

Said Casey: "I bet if the yardmaster caught you he'd give you hell."

The black boy seemed to think this funny. Chuckling, he returned:

"He ain't gonter ketch us, boss. No, suh! Not efn us kin help hit. He'd take hit away fum us fo' his own pusso ıel private self. 'Deed he would. Hit's pow'ful good gin, boss. Want us to fotch you some?"

"None oï that durn stuff for me. You better stay out of the yards with it, too. What's your name?"

"Wallace, please suh."

In some uncertainty, Casey studied him. He said, finally:

"Where'd you come from? You ain't a Kentucky or Tennessee nigger."

Wallace laughed uproariously, exposing shining, white teeth and pink gums mottled with blue.

" 'Scusin' me, suh, you is sho a knowin' young man. No, suh, us don't belong in dese yere parts. Me an' mah Big Bossman is fum de Black Bottom country."

"Way down in Mississippi, huh? Who is your *buckra?*"

Wallace's round bright eyes blinked rapidly. He favored the white boy with a queer look. He replied in an altered tone:

"Cunnel Rance Saunders, suh."

He backed away a step or two. The simian countenance abruptly lighted up again, and again he chuckled knowingly.

" 'Scusin' me, suh, us knows who you is. You is Mist' Casey Jones."

With this surprising revelation, Wallace walked nimbly toward Red Donlin's, clinking some coins in one hand."

"Hey, you! Come to, fella!"

A box car, perilously close, was bearing down upon the engrossed Casey. An angry switchman hanging to step and ladder, had yelled the warning. Mere switchmen no longer held terrors for Casey, however. There was plenty of time to step aside and let the drifting car pass, and, as it did, he grinned impudently and thumbed his nose at the scowling rail.

Next day Casey's almost constant vigil was rewarded. Sadie Carlisle appeared upon the landing again. And she was smoking a cigarette. She was a remarkably handsome woman, he thought. But at this juncture the darky, Wallace, chanting mournfully, came out of Gertie Blake's. An apron of soiled bedticking covered the fore part of him, from chin to ankles. He carried a platter from which he scraped some food for a couple of sleek, lazy looking cats. Not a rat was visible at the moment, the distraction caused Casey to observe.

Sadie Carlisle leaned over the railing and spoke to the darky. It was really remarkable how the sunlight shone upon her coppery hair. Her voice was not harsh or shrill, as were the voices of the other women, but came to Casey with a sort of husky softness.

"Wallace!"

Instantly the song ceased and the darky looked up. His black countenance worked spasmodically in an excess of pleased surprise, his white teeth flashing.

"Yassum, Miss Sadie?"

"Mr. Rance wants to see you tonight," she told him. More soberly, he acknowledged: "Yassum, Miss

Sadie. Thank you, ma'm. Us'll wait fo' him, ma'm."

She added: "At the Silver King. About nine o'clock."

"Efn Cap'n Donlin don' mek us wuhk late us be dere at nine o'clock, Miss Sadie, please ma'm."

She bent down farther, extending the hand that held the half-smoked cigarette.

"Catch!" she bade, and pitched the cigarette.

Wallace attempted to catch it, but it scorched his hand and fell to the ground. Flipping the burnt fingers, he stifled a yelp, then retrieved the butt and stuck it between his bulging lips, puffing vigorously. Sadie Carlisle retreated indoors before he could thank her.

Here came the outraged switchman again, this time riding the dinghy's footboard. And if he could not intimidate Casey, he at least knew how to confuse him with embarrassment.

"You damn' fool!" shouted he. "Don't you know you can't get that gal to come out in the yards? If you want her, go over to her dump."

"Aw, rats!" was the best retort the blushing boy could think of. And his mortification was rendered complete by his voice squeaking on the second word with a very rodent-like effect. Sadie Carlisle could hardly help overhearing what that smart aleck switchman had said, bellowing it out like a bull that way!

When Casey got back into the telegraph office he had time to recover his equilibrium. He stood contemplating Cunny's bowed head until the operator finished taking a message that was clicking in rapidly over the wire; then he casually asked:

"What's the Silver King?"

Cunny looked up sharply but did not answer immediately.

"The Silver King?" he returned at length. "It's a gambling joint—up east of the roundhouse. It's a damn' good place to keep away from."

It was the next day, Sunday, that the shooting occurred.

CHAPTER VIII

COLONEL RANCE SAUNDERS

SUNDAY at Columbus, in and about the railroad yards and the yard offices, was a period of surprising calm; surprising because it was in such striking contrast with the riotous orgies of the night before. This was especially true if Saturday fell upon or near a semi-monthly visit of the paycar. On Saturday nights, Donlin's saloon and the bawdy houses operated under forced draft until the small hours of morning, and then fell into sodden silence.

This Sunday found Casey still under the spell of his exciting new situation; reaction, with a consequent letdown, had not yet begun to set in. Today he determined to take stock of his surroundings.

Accordingly, he wasted no time in his small, cheerless room at Mrs. Riley's boarding-house, which, except for the landlady and her colored girl helper, was occupied solely by employees of the two railroads; and despite the fact that he had not gone to bed until after midnight, he was up with the sun and at the yard offices before Cunny arrived to relieve Charley Spencer.

He had learned that, except for two southbound passenger trains and the corresponding northbound trains, no regular trains passed through the Columbus yards

on this day. There might be a trainload or so of transfer freight stacked in the levee warehouse or loaded in
strings of cars waiting on sidings; if so, traffic would
occupy that status until next day. The dinghy, a con-
verted wood burner, reposed upon a short spur track
near the roundhouse with fire banked. Buck Ewing
was free to be off—with the *Hornets* if there was a
game on the cards—and most of the roundhouse crew,
the switchmen and the office help were away for the
day.

Here was Cunny, now exchanging greetings with the
dour night operator, who hurried away as if late for a
pressing tryst.

"What's the matter with him?" Casey inquired curiously, after the door had closed behind morose Charley
Spencer.

Cunny sighed and wagged his head dolefully, im-
plying that Casey had opened up a subject that was both
painful and sad. He said: "He's in love."

Casey stared. The explanation was inadequate.

Cunny pursued: "There goes the makings of a first-
class brass-pounder, utterly and completely ruint.
Ruint by a flibber-tigibbet of a town gal who ain't worth
dragging in out of the weather."

"Good gosh!" marveled Casey. "Is that what being
in love does to a fella?"

Cunny regarded him severely. "It might," he said
critically, "make your voice settle on whether it's going

to be bass or soprano." Ignoring the youngster's flushed embarrassment, he proceeded to expound:

"If Charley Spencer had to fall in love, he ought to have picked him one of these country cornfeds hereabouts; a sensible gal brought up sound and solid on side-meat and grits and turnip greens and pot liquor. But nope. Not him. He has to go and fall for the giddiest gal in Columbus. And look what it's done to him!"

Casey didn't ask who the girl was. Anyhow, he was too busy thinking to care. Thoughts of the opposite sex had never bothered him much at any time, but Cunny had drawn such an odious picture of Charley Spencer that his mind swiftly reviewed all the girls he had ever known. There weren't many. Starting with Emma, they comprised her circle of playmates, and ended there.

But he was able, without hesitation, to arrive quickly at a sage and mature conclusion, namely: Girls were addlepates, and the less a fellow had to do with them the better it would be for him. Love and its attendant follies and infirmities had no place in the functions of one ordained to become a railroad engineer.

But what if a person fell in love with one of those girls across the tracks, like Buck Ewing had with Garnet? Or the fellow who was Sadie Carlisle's lover? Speculation along this line led to disturbing suggestions that he could not dispose of. So he changed the subject.

"Mr. Cunningham—" he began.

The operator interrupted. "Stop. That's an unfamiliar name. My ear is so attuned to 'Cunny' that I respond but sluggishly if at all to a cognomen more formal and less intimate. I'm Cunny to you, my lad—Cunny to you."

"Well," Casey hesitated in the face of this rhetorical flight, "I was only going to say: If I was a little further along in telegraphy I might take your place on a slack Sunday and let you have a holiday, along with the other fellas."

"You might," was the cautious response. "If you stick to it. And work hard enough."

The boy looked so crestfallen that Cunny went on with added warmth:

"You old squirrel, don't worry. I hear you monkeying with that dummy set. When did you learn to pound out Morse so well?"

Casey was delighted.

"*Is* my sending good? Before I came here I already knew the code, but I'd never had any practice sending."

Cunny assumed a severe air. Shaking a finger in the novice's face, he said: "Get this, young fella. Sending is the easiest part of telegraphing. How soon you going to learn to receive? *That's* the question."

"You don't think—now—do you?—it's going to take me eight months to be a ham?"

"Let's hope not. You're pretty thick-headed though, for an ape your size."

With spirits considerably·elevated, Casey set out for
the roundhouse. He tried to whistle *Oh, Susannah!*
and was not a whit discouraged by his inability to carry
even so simple a tune. He had a feeling that it wasn't
going to take him long to master telegraphy; Cunny's
manner rather than his words had crystallized this feeling into conviction. As Cunny assured Lem Miller,
later in the day, he had the knack. Major Hosford
might find him a paying job before all his $100 was
gone.

Striding over the cinders, whistling shrilly and happily, he came upon the darky Wallace. It was a transformed Wallace. Casey had to stare hard before he
recognized him. Wallace was togged out in a Prince
Albert coat with breeches to match and a stiff derby.
The garments were of expensive texture and not so
long ago had been of fashionable cut; but for their
present wearer the breeches were so much too long that
they hung round his shanks in folds, the coat tails almost dragged upon the cinders, and only Wallace's
protruding ears prevented the derby from eclipsing his
monkeylike face. Coat, pants and hat alike had faded
to a soft, uniform plum shade.

Casey's exuberant spirits found vent in a cordial salu-
tation.

"Well, dog my cats, if it ain't Wallace! I thought
first you was a parson or—or an undertaker or a bar-
tender. Where's the preachin' at? Or is it a buryin'?"

Highly pleased by this recognition of his sartorial

elegance, the boy's black features were convulsed, the little round eyes became dancing sparks of jet.

"Howdy, Mist' Casey Jones. Us is gonter Sunday meetin'."

"Do tell! Primitive Baptist, I'll bet."

Wallace writhed and laughed in an ecstacy of delight.

"Yessuh. You is sho a knowin' young man. Us wushups wid de Beekum Light o' Zion flock. Us is deacon."

Casey tried to appear properly impressed, but he couldn't help asking:

"Tell me, Deacon—how did you come by that suit of clothes? And that hat? I never see anything so splendiferous."

Wallace cackled.

"Splen—splen—a" essayed the enraptured darky. "Whut's dat fine mouf-ful er word agin, Mist' Casey, please suh?"

"Splendiferous? But that don't come up to the way you look today, Deke. I should have said you're *magnificento* splendiferous."

Wallace's soft voice rose in as near a whoop as it could attain; a subdued, flute-like flourish that was remarkably expressive without in the least disturbing the Sabbath quiet.

"Who-o-o-ee! Us'll have to tell Cunnel Mont Savage whut gimme dese hyar clo's 'bout dat. My! Won't he be tickled!"

"Colonel who?"

"Cunnel Mont Savage, please suh. He's Bossman at de Silver King."

"Better not," Casey cautioned. "He might want 'em back."

After they separated, Casey's pace slowed down; he fell silent. *That* was something to think about. That little nigger, coming out of the hell holes and sinks of iniquity, all togged out, to attend the Beacon Light of Zion church. A deacon, too.

Sunday was a fine day to visit the roundhouse. The layover locomotives would be in their stalls, and a friendly hostler maybe wouldn't object if he looked them over. The hostler, a good-natured individual, turned out to be more friendly than Casey had anticipated. He yearned for somebody—anybody—to talk with. He even permitted Casey to climb in and out of the various cabs at will, and at least seemed to enjoy answering the volley of questions fired at him. His loquacity revealed an unbridled imagination that made the boy suspicious of most of the answers. But what of that? Casey was discovering things for himself, learning things in his own way. What a gold mine of opportunities! Hereafter he would put in most of his spare time at the roundhouse.

The forenoon slid by so quickly that he was astonished when the hostler abruptly broke off talking and went to dinner.

And now Casey decided to rejoin Cunny at the yard

offices instead of going the few steps to Mrs. Riley's for his own dinner. Back along the yard tracks he trudged, his thoughts full of his adventures at the roundhouse. He could have had no premonition that every step was bringing him gradually closer to an episode that was to affect his immediate future in no slight degree.

The day was fairly saturated with Sabbath calm. He saw nothing more of Wallace, nor did he encounter anybody else. There was not one thing to intrude upon his happy day-dreaming.

He passed the telegraph office bay window through which he saw Cunny, comfortably propped back with feet on desk, evidently snoozing. Farther back in the room he could make out the figure of the agent, Lem Miller, moving about.

All at once an infernal din broke out—three or four women frantically screaming. Indeed, the outcry rose to such a pitch of stark, agonizing terror that Casey, startled beyond words, stopped dead in his tracks, sensible of a most unpleasant pringling along his spine and over his scalp. His bewildered wits automatically located the uproar in Sadie Carlisle's place, where the closely shaded windows provided no clue as to what the commotion was all about.

There was no time to adjust scattered wits, either. The door off the landing banged open, and a man, hatless and coatless, plunged out and fairly threw himself down the wooden steps, as if all the demons of Hell were about to seize him.

Directly behind him came a second man, a hand under his coat tail tugging at something in his hip pocket. Blood streamed down the second man's face and stained the front of his white shirt and sprigged, fawn-colored waistcoat.

Half-way down the stairway, the fugitive vaulted the railing, stumbled, recovered his balance, and sped desperately toward the front of the building.

Something flashed dazzlingly in the sunlight as the pursuer halted on the steps. He deliberately aimed a revolver at the other. The weapon cracked, and dust spurted ahead of the runner. Then the pursuer, in turn, raced on down to the ground, and swung round for another shot, swaying forward drunkenly, holding pistol in both hands.

Right then Casey realized that the next instant was going to place his life in jeopardy—if that crazy fella fired again. The action was spaced by split seconds. No human could have striven more madly to reach a spot of safety than did the fugitive. The pursuer, now on the ground, the other fleeing toward the front of Donlin's, Casey paralyzed where he stood, were so aligned that the boy was directly within range of the flashing, sinister revolver.

And just as the fugitive virtually hurled himself around the sheltering corner of the brick, the other fired again. The bullet spat with an ugly sound directly in front of Casey, glanced, and whined past his head. He ducked instinctively—after the bullet had passed—and when he looked again the first man had disappeared.

Now Sadie Carlisle was on the steps, the sunlight shining on her coppery hair. Both hands held her encumbering skirts high, generously revealing shapely legs in flesh-tinted silken hose, and she, too, ran down the stairs as fast as her high-heeled slippers would permit.

Close enough, though, to be right at the second man's heels. Her hold of the filmy skirt folds released, and she held out her right hand to him and spoke. Her soft, husky voice was not raised; it betrayed no tremor but carried a distinct note of authority.

"Give me that pistol, Rance."

He half turned and pointed the weapon at her bosom. Only a matter of inches lay between her and the muzzle; between her and death. So desperately earnest was the man's bloodstained countenance that Casey chilled with horror. He fully expected to hear another shot and to see the woman crumple to the ground.

But she laughed—a hard, mirthless laugh. It was plain that she was wholly unafraid. Her tone and mien were boldly contemptuous.

"You haven't the nerve to shoot me," she told him. "As if I cared!" And she repeated: "Give me that pistol."

A long tense moment, then slowly he lowered the weapon and put it in her waiting hand.

And the whole thing ended with a high relief of comedy. Gertie Blake's side door opened, and there stood Gertie herself, her fat body encased in an extremely scanty, extremely dirty negligee. Wisps of stringy hair hung round her coarse, inflamed face. She weaved unsteadily in the doorway: she was very drunk. At the top of her voice she shrieked, at no one in particular:

"Shoot the bastard! Kill him! The son of a bitch ain't got no friends nohow!"

Some unseen power in the background jerked her forcibly into the house. The door slammed, and no more was heard from Gertie Blake.

A laugh went up from the little knot of men who were gathering from—nobody could tell where. Some of them hooted and called for an encore from Gertie. The crowd was swelling. Excitement ran high. And under cover of the diversion, Sadie contrived to steer the would-be assassin to the foot of the stairs, and somehow persuaded him to ascend and to return with her to her apartment.

Scarcely two minutes had elapsed since the first shrieks of the terror-stricken girls rent the air. Now, abruptly, like the lowering of a curtain, the Sabbath peace and calm were restored.

Casey drew a long breath and felt his taut, aching muscles relax. He wondered what the sequel to such an affair might be. Well, possibly he might be a witness to that, too; for anything so deadly in earnest was bound to have a sequel.

"Rance," he muttered, remembering the name. "Why, that must be Wallace's Big Bossman, Rance Saunders."

CHAPTER IX

SPECULATION

IF A revolver had suddenly commenced barking in the main yard offices Monday morning, it wouldn't have caused more of a sensation than what actually did happen. It was no other than the quiet, gentle mannered Mr. Miller who created the furor. He blew up, in a manner of speaking, when Casey Jones discovered why the semaphore would not work.

But a number of things led up to the explosion, some of which had their origin in an indefinite past; causes that were cumulative over a long period of time. What followed Sunday's affair, however, touched off the agent's pent up feelings.

The shooting, as one may well believe, was foremost in the minds of everybody and, as work permitted, was the sole topic of conversation.

What had happened over there at Sadie Carlisle's yesterday morning?

There were as many versions of the affair as there were tongues in the office, each individual wanting to convey the impression that he alone had the inside story but that it would be indiscreet if not downright dangerous to divulge all that he knew. Casey was a focal point of interest because he had seen more of the actual shooting than any one else; but he was a stranger in Columbus, and only a kid into the bargain, so he could not be expected to have knowledge of probable motives.

"You say the bullet zipped right past your head?" he was asked for possibly the hundredth time. "Wasn't you scared stiff, though!"

To which he would reply rather sheepishly: "I reckon I thought it whizzed past closer than it did."

The gabble grew tiresome. After an hour or so Casey's attention was directed to what was being sent over one of the commercial wires. To be able to close one's ears to all extraneous matters, no matter how exciting, and concentrate upon what the telegraph sounder is clicking out becomes ingrained in every operator worth his salt.

Why should Casey be interested in the shooting? He didn't know any of the persons involved; they were not, he might have moralized if he were older, the type of citizen that it would be desirable to know. So he slid into the extra chair at the instrument desk and, armed with a pencil, bent over a pad of paper and endeavored to catch the rapid staccato message, jotting down every letter or word that he could read. He had been assured that this was the only way to learn to receive.

Yet, despite his disinterested attitude and detachment, whenever Sadie Carlisle's name was mentioned as a factor in the shooting, he found himself listening— to such an extent had the woman ensnared his curiosity.

Among the conflicting versions, jealousy over her was advanced as the cause of the affray. This, on its face, seemed reasonable. Casey gathered—as he already had inferred—that the man who did the shooting was Rance Saunders; but he learned for the first time that the unwilling target was Mont Savage, Bossman at the Silver King, donor of Wallace's outlandish Sunday-go-to-meeting attire.

This theory was disputed, however, by one which found several supporters. The man who offered it did not openly say so but hinted that "slick handling" of the cards in a poker game had been the cause, that fella Saunders being the "slick" one. A fight started, during which Savage, getting the worst of it, grabbed up a handy beer bottle and clubbed his adversary over the head with it. The sanguinary details observed by Casey lent weight to this theory.

And the jealousy motive was still further discredited. Sadie Carlisle was generally recognized as Rance Saunder's woman—for hadn't the pair come up from Mississippi together and remained together ever since? —and Mont Savage had fallen hard for that new blonde from St. Louis—the one known as Goldie. Everybody ought to know that. The fight became serious only when Savage resorted to the beer bottle and Saunders went for his gun, which caught in his pistol pocket.

Thus speculation ran on without certain result.

But Casey wondered. He could not wipe out of

memory the bitter expression on Rance Saunders' blood-stained face when he pointed the pistol at Sadie Carlisle's bosom. It was improbable that the woman had accused him of cheating—at any rate, not at cards. What, then, could have been the motive for his bitter anger at her? There was a terrible long moment, the boy knew, when her life hung by a thread.

Cunny, too, had work to do. He was in his own chair, with its dilapidated horsehair and leather seat-pad, right alongside Casey. For a couple of extras were being made up, and there was a northbound extra out of Jackson, to say nothing of the regular trains both ways, all of which had to be watched and reported to the transfer-line dispatchers and train masters, south-bound trains to be given running schedules from Columbus. It was things like this that kept an operator busy.

But Cunny had time to steal a glimpse now and then of the lad beside him and note what he was doing. During a momentary lull, he remarked, aside:

"Fella, how do you do it? You got almost all of that last message. The commercial wire, too!"

The concluding note of astonishment was evoked by the fact that matter sent over the commercial wire was composed of highly technical abbreviations and shot along at a speed which only a skilled operator, and one familiar with railroad business, could be expected to read and transcribe smoothly.

His surprise at the novice's quickness to learn was

erased by a vexatious matter that demanded immediate attention. He was tugging impatiently at one of the semaphore controls.

"Damn that semaphore!" Cunny ripped out. "It's still stuck. What the hell's the matter with it?" He stood up to wrestle with the obstinate control wire.

Lem Miller intervened.

"Casey," he directed, "find a ladder and see if you can fix that thing." To which Cunny added: "Take along the oil can and give the pulleys a squirt of cylinder oil."

One of Casey's duties was to keep the lamps filled and trimmed and to light them at sundown, so he didn't have to hunt for the ladder. The semaphore was not hard to reach, and it didn't take Casey more than two seconds to discover what the trouble was and to remove it. Cunny, watching from below through the window, now easily pulled the arm to "stop" position.

Casey reentered the office rather breathlessly.

"Look!" he cried. He held out a hand and exhibited his trophy.

"Looks like a mashed car-door seal."

"Car-door seal my eye!" Casey scoffed at the suggestion. "That's the bullet that almost drilled a hole in me yesterday."

The others stared. The lead slug had flattened against the inside of the metal pulley housing. Movement of the wire control had finally loosened it, and it had dropped in such a way as to wedge firmly between the small wheel and the metal frame, locking the former.

Here it was that the explosion came. All eyes turned to Lem Miller.

The agent had thumped with such violence upon a desk top that paper-weights and ink bottles rattled and banged together. His eyes blazed and his face was pale with indignation.

"That's the last straw!" he shouted, striding to and fro and hammering his right fist into the other palm for emphasis. "That's the final insult! Things have come to a pretty pass if those hell holes can damage railroad property and get away with it! Are we to go on tolerating the jeopardizing of our very lives by those sinks of iniquity, with their brazen defiance of law and decency? No!" he thundered. "A thousand times NO! They got to be destroyed! *They got to go!*" With unrestrained fury, he seized his hat and hurried away.

A long interval of silence followed the eruption. The first break came from the direction of the train-register shelf, where Arch Frazier, engineer, and Bide Cole, conductor, were waiting unnoticed for their clearance for No. 3.

"Whe-e-e-ew!" gushed from Frazier, much like steam from a petcock. "Did you hear that! What's biting the old man? Has he gone crazy?"

The others wagged their heads helplessly, too dumfounded to speak until Cunny found voice.

"I never see him cut up that bad before," said he in a

tone hushed by awe. "It's the worst ever." Then, with reviving animation: "But I recognize the symptom. I betcha we're in for another reform wave."

After excitement had simmered down and No. 3 had been sent on its way southward, Casey asked Cunny:

"Won't the Town Marshal do something about the shooting?"

Cunny gave vent to a violent snort of scorn.

"Them no account crooked bastards? If you only half-knew Hank Weaver and Tick Torbett you wouldn't ask such a fool question. I bet they haven't even heard there's been a shootin'."

Weaver and Torbett were, respectively, the Town Marshal and his assistant.

The boy, in his innocence, harbored an idea that all law-abiding citizens enjoyed the protection of an invulnerable shield known as The Law. Lacking the vocabulary to express himself clearly on the subject, he asked:

"Ain't the Marshal supposed to—to—well, sort of protect folks like us from folks like them across the tracks?"

Cunny regarded him pityingly.

"Kid," said he, "you got a lot to learn." Then he became cynical. "You haven't ever seen any of them chippies or their pimps and macks bothering us, have you? Well, you won't. They pay for their privileges, and there's an understanding that they aren't to cross the line."

"Line?" echoed Casey, staring around as if to discover some conspicuously visible mark. "What line?"

"Why, as long as they go on coughing up to the officers they can do about as they please short of murder. If a rail or some damn' fool gets himself killed in one of their joints, the sheriff comes boiling down from the county seat and makes things as hot as hell for whoever did it. It's not playing square. In a case like that somebody is even apt to get hung. But things get straightened out. The fiddlers commence fiddling again, the dancers start dancing, and everybody goes to whooping 'er up like a lot of maniacs as though nothing had ever happened."

Casey fished the mutilated bullet from a pocket and held it in his palm.

"Suppose this had hit me?" he queried.

"The world," opined Cunny, "would have lost the greenest thing that ever crawled out of the tall weeds. If that bullet had clipped you—you being connected with the railroad in a sort of way—maybe some action would have been taken. I don't know. You can take this as gospel, though, sonny: as far as the law is concerned, you've heard the last of what happened at Sadie Carlisle's."

Even as Cunny predicted, affairs settled down to their customary routine, and it appeared that he knew what he was talking about. For a night or two the dives across the way were comparatively dark and quiet, then by degrees restraint was laid aside and wickedness was flaunted as openly as before.

It is necessary, however, to return to Monday morning and to Lem Miller. It was late afternoon when the agent returned to his duties. He had cooled down, of course, but a purposeful light gleamed from under his shaggy, grizzled eyebrows. His jaw was grimly set, and although he had little to say about anything and nothing at all about what had upset him, it was obvious that something momentous was hatching.

With Cunny's help, he got off two reports: one to the Division Superintendent, the other to the Maintenance of Way Superintendent. The operator privately confided to Casey that the brass hats would get the idea from the reports that the Columbus yard offices had been subjected to heavy artillery fire, and the fellas who worked there had been made targets by bands of villainous sharpshooters. Cunny no doubt exaggerated, but Miller could be depended on to couch the reports in sufficiently strong language.

The shooting affray and its attendant excitements did more than anything else to accustom Casey Jones to his new surroundings. As the novelty wore off, he found it increasingly easier to forget outside attractions and to occupy himself with learning telegraphy and its application to the business of railroading.

He did not mind serving as errand boy occasionally, especially when he became alert enough to distinguish between legitimate missions and practical jokes. After he had been sent on an endless parade over the town in quest of red oil for the signal lanterns and, another time, for a left-hand monkey-wrench, he grew canny and failed to bite when Sam Penny, the freight house clerk, wanted him to go to Gus Barlow's hardware store—a two-mile walk—for a "circular square."

"Fella," he declared, "I'm here to learn. If you can show me how to use a circular square in runnin' a railroad or handlin' freight, I'll get you one."

Penny, who was not resourceful, was unable to carry on, so the laugh in this instance was on him.

In a surprisingly short time Casey had made a place for himself in the yard offices, and late at night, when main line traffic was off the division, nobody objected when he carried on halting conversations over one of the wires with such operators up and down the line as he could engage in this manner. They liked to kid him, calling him "ham" and the like, but they would "talk" to him, and that was the main thing.

He liked best of all to talk with the night man at Cayce. Thus he could indirectly keep in touch with his folks.

Late one night Charley Spencer surprised Casey by asking:

"Say, kid, do you know where I could borrow a good sized valise?"

Casey's thoughts flashed to the shiny old patent-leather valise under his bed; to Steve Gowdy holding it aloft in wonderment that it should be so light, so empty.

"Why, yes," he replied, "I reckon so. You aiming to go away somewhere?"

Spencer did not answer directly, and Casey did not notice the evasion. Spencer was assuring him:

"I want it for a friend of mine. I guarantee good care will be taken of it. If anything happens to it I'll make it good."

In the quiet hour before daybreak, Casey went to his room and got the valise. He dumped its few contents upon the bed and hurried back to the office with it. Spencer surveyed the unattractive object with obvious misgiving but at last expressed doubtful approval.

"I guess it'll do," said he. "And I don't know how to thank you."

"Forget it," said Casey.

Charley Spencer took up Casey's valise and presented a picture of one about to embark upon a journey.

"Things are pretty quiet," Spencer pointed out. "I sha'n't be gone more than a minute or so." He went out, taking the valise.

He was as good as his word. And in the short remaining period before seven o'clock, Casey wondered and speculated until his head fairly ached. Who wanted his valise and why? Where had Charley Spencer taken it that he could get back so quickly? Across the yard tracks? Incredible. In the long steady look the pair of them had exchanged, Casey had seen something that he had not seen before. He had, for the first time, begun to get acquainted with the night-trick man.

Spencer's eyes were blue, steady in their regard; the eyes of a square guy. Maybe Spencer, with his stocky frame and coarse, unruly sandy hair, was not very good to look at, but he was a man who could be relied on. Casey was as much astonished by arriving at these conclusions as by anything else connected with the incident. And, gal or no gal, he had to give the fella credit for knowing his job and sticking to it. That old hoss Cunny was too free with his opinions, anyhow.

Casey did not spend all his waking hours over the telegraph instruments. There were games with the *Hornets*, and his prowess on the diamond was bringing him fame throughout the region. Twice the *Hornets* journeyed to Cayce to play the *Dreadnaughts*. On these occasions he visited with the home folks, all of whom now called him Casey—except his mother. To her he was still Luther.

His Sundays were usually spent at the roundhouse among the locomotives and with the talkative engine hostler Winkler Jones and with engineers, who were secretly astonished by his knowledge of locomotives.

A whole week had passed without Casey's voice once evincing a disposition to crack. Then ten days elapsed without vocal catastrophe. By the end of this period he had developed a quality of intonated utterance that permanently registered somewhere between bass and baritone, which if not as hoarse and tattered as Steve Gowdy's had been, was not displeasing to the ear. It gave him added confidence. He kept a lookout for the smart aleck switchman, hoping the fellow would bawl him out again so that he could tell him to go to hell and make it sound as if he meant it.

A revival meeting was in full swing, Lem Miller having been the prime mover in launching it on its way with the object of cleaning up the viciousness that flourished adjacent to the yards.

Charley Spencer, apparently taking him at his word to "forget it," did not fetch back his valise, nor did he refer to it.

CHAPTER X

WHIPSAWED

IT IS remarkable that the unsophisticated boy became a proficient telegraph operator in such a short time. The trainmaster was frankly skeptical. Whoever heard of anybody mastering telegraphy so quickly? But the annual grain rush was under way; the road was crowded with traffic; operators were needed, and they were scarce. With many doubts and misgivings in their minds, the dispatcher and trainmaster allowed him to work one night at C-Y yard office. Necessity governed this decision.

All night long extras were heading south laden with wheat, and as many were arriving from the south with long strings of empties to be filled once more. For, as Cunny explained, the grain rush was on. From the huge granary of the great Middle West, the golden flood of wheat was beginning to move south through St. Louis and on to the seaboard for export. The Mobile & Ohio was receiving its share for overseas shipment out of Mobile.

"Casey," Lem Miller asked him on one of the busy evenings, "you reckon you could help Spencer tonight?"

The boy's heart leaped. This meant that he was now recognized as an operator who could hold down a job—a job as difficult and exacting as the C-Y yard office!

"Sure I can," he answered without hesitation. "Just let me have a chance."

Miller hesitated. The boy was so young and inexperienced. But he had watched him taking fast, abbreviated commercial business and doing it easily, and C-Y needed an additional operator until the stress and strain of the busy season eased up.

"Well," Miller decided, "something's got to be done. The trainmaster says he hasn't an extra operator available."

When Charley Spencer came on duty at seven o'clock that night, Casey was already seated at the half-circle table in the big bay window under a huge hanging brass oil lamp that might have served as well for heating as for lighting purposes. The yellow glow from its tubular wick shone through a nimbus of gnats, mosquitoes and other winged insects, which annoyed the operators by raining upon the napes of their necks and upon the desk.

Armed with an agate stylus, a carbon manifold before him, Casey was busy transcribing a 31 order for No. 53, second-class southbound train, to meet No. 30 at Rutherford, No. 30 to take the siding. No. 30 likewise was a second-class train, running so far behind that if it didn't arrive soon it would be annulled.

He took the order smoothly and swiftly, repeated it back to the dispatcher and received the official "12 complete J. A. P., 6:55 P.M." J. A. P. was the train-master's initial signature.

Lem Miller turned away with a sigh of profound relief, while the boy experienced a feeling of inex-pressible joy and satisfaction. A regular operator in one of the road's busiest and most important offices! He was figuratively sitting on the Pearly Gates swing-ing his feet.

But, lo, the very next night an extra operator showed up to relieve him, armed with an order from "Jap" Pegler, the trainmaster! Surprise gave way to disap-pointment and humiliation to hot anger as Casey pon-dered this gross injustice. He had gone in as a pinch hitter, produced the winning run and was rewarded by removal from the game. All that night the boy nursed his grievances against the M. & O., Pegler and the world in general.

Next day he put in his usual time at the station, but he could not refrain from voicing aloud the protest that was constantly struggling for expression.

"I'm going to get me out of this rotten town and over to a railroad where ability is appreciated. That ham from Jackson is a drunken bum. Just let him stay here long enough and see what happens!" He ex-pressed his opinion of the M. & O. in language that was picturesquely profane.

"No, no, Casey," Lem Miller objected. "Don't do anything rash, now. I can't tell you too much but I can drop a hint. Major Hosford has plans for you. He's the big brass hat on the division."

Again Casey had to stare at the little agent. It was sometimes difficult to make him out.

"You mean," the boy said at last, "he's going to give me a job firing?"

"I can't say," returned Miller, "but your position here is more assured than you realize."

"Boy, boy, such language!" Cunny uttered, pretending to be shocked beyond words. "Lad, you need some sort of saving grace. I never realized you were so hardened, that you were sunk so deep in depravity. You need the ministrations of the Reverend Joshua Honeycutt."

Casey, brooding over his own soreness, was not heeding. Lem Miller chided Cunny.

"Don't make light of so serious a subject."

"I ain't," Cunny protested. "I'm simply trying to persuade this wicked, long-legged galliwumpus from the backwoods to go with me and seek salvation."

"What in hell do you mean?" demanded Casey darkly.

"There you go again," retorted Cunny. "It's not hell but heaven I have in mind. Since you been fired off this job let's you and I go to camp meeting."

This was the first Casey had heard of the revival. He assented when the day man again urged him to "Come along and forget your troubles."

Neither of them noticed that the darky, Wallace, was loitering in the shadows of the freight house platform when they emerged, nor that he followed them furtively as they proceeded toward the camp meeting.

CHAPTER XI

SAWDUST TRAIL

CASEY and Cunny chatted seriously but amiably in the moon-lit dusk on their way to the tent where the revival was being held. As they neared the entrance they came upon a rich looking turnout: a glistening two-seated surrey to which was hitched a span of thorough-bred chestnut geldings. Casey clutched his companion's arm, jerking him to a halt.

"Who's rig is that?"

Cunny was startled.

"Why?" he asked.

But Casey could only repeat, "Who's rig is that?"

"Well," said Cunny, "if it means anything to you, that's Colonel Mose Terris's turnout. It's his daughter that Charley Spencer is so crazy about."

Casey's dilapidated old patent-leather valise reposed on the back seat of the surrey.

"See that valise? That's mine! Charley Spencer borrowed it."

Cunny considered this information. Then he commenced laughing.

"I'll be doggoned!" he exclaimed. "Spencer and Loutha Terris are going to elope. Tonight. In the old man's prize rig." Then another thought came to

103

him. "Who," he concluded, "is going to work C-Y tonight?"

"Yeh," returned Casey, "who?   It won't be me."

"Listen, young fella.   If Spencer and Miss Terris really do elope tonight, it means he's not on the job. The paycar was here today and he's got his check. So——"

"So what?" said Casey.

"The call-boys will be out trying to run me down tonight, and I don't mean to be found."

At this instant Cunny performed an extraordinary vanishing act, disappearing as if by magic in the crowd at the tent entrance.   This peculiar conduct was instantly explained when Casey felt a tug at his coat tail and turned to gaze down into the familiar face of one of the call-boys—a little fellow, younger than Casey—known as Half Pint.   The boy was panting from his exertions of worming through the crowd.   Cunny, of course, had seen the boy before the latter had seen him.

"Gosh!" gasped Half Pint.   "I been hunting all over creation for you, Casey Jones.   You're wanted at C-Y right off.   They want Cunny, too.   You seen him?"

"I saw him disappear just like a puff of smoke and I haven't seen him since.   You're good if you can find him tonight.   Wait a second."

Casey considered the situation.   With Spencer failing to show up and both Cunny and himself away, full responsibility for running busy C-Y tonight would fall upon old Lem Miller, for there was no extra operator on hand. Still incensed and resentful, Casey wanted more than anything in the world to ignore this summons. But there was poor old Lem, not too robust, having to work a 24-hour trick. This turned the scale. He directed Half Pint:

"Hurry back and tell Mr. Miller I'll be along in a jiffy."

Half Pint in turn disappeared in the throng.

Casey set out to follow the youngster. At the outer fringes of the crowd a figure confronted him, so suddenly and unexpectedly that it gave him a start.

"Wallace!" he exclaimed. "You been following me! What for?"

The little darky's manner was fraught with mystery. He beckoned Casey to accompany him off among the shadows of adjacent trees.

Wallace fumbled inside his shirt and drew forth what appeared to be a small bundle of cloth. He sank to one knee and commenced unwinding the folds. Then something flashed and glittered in the moonlight, and Casey found himself gazing at a bright and shining revolver.

Casey's fascinated inspection of the weapon ended when he drew a long breath and looked up to encounter the Negro's anxious gaze.

"Wallace," he said with bated breath, "that's the pistol your bossman tried to shoot Mr. Savage with. How come you got it? What you going to do with it?"

CHAPTER XII

RECOGNITION

THE colored boy explained that Miss Sadie had given him the pistol and told him to hide it. "But," he said, "whar at *kin* us hide hit? A nigger ain't got no business totin' a weapon lak dis hyar. You keep hit please, Mist' Casey."

Thus Casey Jones came into possession of a weapon that was to figure shortly in a real tragedy.

Casey didn't push the office door open. He kicked it open. What a contrast with the fear and trembling that beset him when first he stood before this same door such a short time before!

Lem Miller presented a haggard appearance and any impudence of which Casey might have delivered himself was at once discouraged by the agent's weary figure. Miller was plainly relieved to see the boy. He had already received a message from the train-master authorizing Casey to work as relief operator at C-Y that night and indefinitely.

"I reckon," said Casey, "that Charley Spencer has gone for good—he and his girl."

"Yes," said Lem Miller solemnly. "He left a note. Said you would hear from him later. But here's good news." He handed Casey two messages.

The boy's first glance at the signatures showed him that they were from Major Hosford, the division superintendent. The texts of the messages gave him a thrill.

One was an order for him to report at the office of the Division superintendent at Jackson on the 28th instant, and the other was an order to conductors and engineers to deadhead him from Columbus to Jackson.

"Hot ziggety!" he cried. "My chance has come. Me, I'm on my way to an engine cab!" Once again he perched on the Pearly Gates.

"I hope your wish is coming true," said Miller.

"And looky, Mr. Miller," the boy went on excitedly, "whether a relief or a regular operator comes or not, I'm on my way to Jackson—the 28th. That's day after tomorrow."

Alone in C-Y office all that night, it was with the early gray of dawn that Casey espied the lifeless figure on the outside wooden steps across at Sadie Carlisle's. Excitement followed the discovery that the body was that of Rance Saunders. He had been slain by a crushing blow on top of the head. Suspicion turned naturally to Mont Savage, but the man had not been seen in the vicinity since the day of the earlier imbroglio. When Casey was leaving the office at seven in the morning he was accosted by none other than Sadie Carlisle.

"You're Casey Jones," said the woman.

Casey could only nod assent. She went on:

"I want the pistol that Wallace Saunders turned over to you."

The boy assured her that he would deliver it to her as soon as he could hurry to his room and return. Then he found himself unexpectedly blurting:

"You aiming to kill somebody with it?"

The woman's hazel eyes scrutinized him for some moments before she replied.

"What a question! The pistol is mine. I want it." And within a few minutes Casey had turned it over to her.

Excitement over the order to appear at the division superintendent's office and preparation for his transfer caused him to temporarily forget the incident.

Casey wrapped up his few extra clothes and other personal effects and went downstairs to pay his board and room and bid goodbye to Mrs. Riley. The kindly landlady had won a place in the boy's affections and had become, in turn, exceedingly fond of her gangling young boarder. The shedding of several motherly tears preceded Casey's dash to the station where he was happy to learn that Bose Lashley would be the eagle eye on the extra south and had invited him to ride to Jackson in the locomotive's cab.

At Jackson, the hub of West Tennessee, the Mobile and Ohio crossed the Illinois Central at an angle that might be represented by the letter X, and the city was an important junction and transfer point for passen-

gers between the two railroads. Casey was curious to
inspect the M. & O. north yards and passenger station
at Jackson—a layout which had excited his interest
ever since he had been at Columbus—so he left Lashley at this point about three miles from the lower
freight terminal, intending to ride a succeeding passenger train the rest of the way to the roundhouse
where he was to meet Bose, and then on to the division
offices.

As he was about to board the train at the station following his inspection he was surprised to see Wallace
Saunders hop from the Jim Crow car and hurry up to
the baggage car. Wallace was arrayed in the misfit
suit that Mont Savage had given him. Then he saw
Sadie Carlisle, heavily veiled. He recognized her by
her carriage.

Their presence was explained at once. A box was
about to be transferred from the newly arrived M. & O.
train to an Illinois Central train, due to depart southward in a few minutes. The woman, recognizing
Casey, requested him to lend a hand in the transfer.
He complied, of course, but with no great relish for the
job.

"It's Mr. Saunders, I reckon?" he inquired politely
of Sadie Carlisle.

"Yes," she told him. "We—Wallace and I—are
taking him back to the old home in Mississippi for
burial in the family cemetery."

Sadie Carlisle hurried back to her car, while Wallace lingered a moment, scrutinizing Casey, his face working spasmodically, more like a monkey's than ever.

"Good-by, boy," said Casey with a degree of earnestness, for he had grown to like the little darky. "Your big Bossman came to a bad end, but when you get back to the Black Bottom country you'll find plenty of jobs. I reckon I'll not see you soon again. Maybe sometime."

Wallace favored the white boy with one of the penetrating looks that always puzzled the latter. He said solemnly:

"Who knows how soon, Mist' Casey? Us knows it won't be long before us meets again. Good-bye, suh."

All that had happened in connection with Sadie Carlisle, Rance Saunders and Wallace had deeply affected the impressionable boy.

Casey found Bose Lashley waiting for him at the roundhouse, and they proceeded to division headquarters where they were much surprised to learn that Major Hosford had completed all details affecting Casey's immediate future.

"How tall are you, Casey?" the Major asked after the first words of greeting.

"Six foot, three inches, sir," the boy informed him. "Is that goin' to be a black mark against me?"

"No, my lad. But your size disguises your true age. You are going to be a whale of a man when you stop growing, and we need that type on our railroad. You can easily pass as one who has reached his majority, but I have obtained a minority waiver from your parents. You can't go on a locomotive immediately, but I will give you a job braking. In that way you will learn the road thoroughly, from Mobile to Columbus. We'll see how you succeed in that line of the work, then consider whether you are qualified to take a place in an engine cab."

Braking in those days was difficult and hazardous, for there were no air-brakes and no brakes of any kind on the locomotives. Much depended upon the brakeman's ability to manipulate the hand-brake on each car. The work was doubly dangerous and disagreeable during the freezing months of winter. Furthermore the cars were equipped with pin and link couplers, direct cause of many lost fingers and maimed hands when the "shack" or brakeman was fortunate enough to escape being thrown beneath the car wheels.

Although it had never occurred to Casey that in attaining his great ambition he would be called upon to flip the rear end of freight trains, he quickly recognized the logic of the Major's plans for his future.

"This means I'm on my way to a job of firing?"

"If you make good, yes," Major Hosford assured him.

"When do I start?" Casey demanded.

CHAPTER XIII

LOVE AT FIRST SIGHT

IT WAS arranged that Casey was to take a run south next day, from Jackson to Whistler, some five and a half miles north of Mobile. At Whistler were located the Mobile & Ohio yards and shops. The run, of course, was primarily for the purpose of enabling him to learn the road between the two terminals and to familiarize himself with the duties of a "shack" on a busy run.

After they had left Major Hosford, Bose Lashley slapped Casey on the back, exclaiming:

"Congratulations, you old brass pounder, now you are a full-fledged rail. Hungry?"

"I can eat half a cow," Casey averred earnestly.

"I'm going to take you to my boarding house and introduce you to the best eats south of St. Louis," the engineer assured him. "Mrs. Brady's boarding house is famous among all rails, and I hope I can find a stall for you there—one at least big enough for you to head into and back out of. And, young fella, she has a daughter—the prettiest girl you ever set eyes on. Only sixteen."

The eats appealed to Casey, but the pretty daughter

112

left him cold. All he said in response to this was, "Huh!" registering complete indifference.

Upon their arrival at Mrs. Brady's, a typical railroad boarding house, Lashley proceeded straight to the parlor, where, startled by their unannounced entrance, a young girl rose quickly from a piano stool and stood for a moment in confusion until she recognized the engineer. Then the startled look vanished, and a smile transfigured her strikingly pretty face, glorifying her lovely gray eyes.

Next her regard met Casey's. During a long moment something terrific flashed and shuttled between them, but the only utterance Casey could make was a short stammering acknowledgement of Bose Lashley's introduction.

Precisely what followed, Casey never could have told. But his emotions can be explained by the statement that he was deeply, desperately in love for the first time in his life. For the last time, too, as it turned out. The loveliness of Jane Brady had swept all his foundations from beneath him. Spiritually and emotionally, he was abject.

It was a case of love at first sight. Naturally one would expect the inevitable outcome to such a situation, but a considerable period of time elapsed before Casey Jones plucked up courage to tell this lovely creature that he loved her and wanted her for his wife. That first night at the Brady boarding house the boy spent in something akin to a daze.

So it was with mixed feelings that the stripling hied himself to the yards next morning in anticipation of his first run. In the division superintendent's office he was informed: "We're always short of men on the South End at this season. That's where you're headed for, buddy. Here's your passport. See Murphy— door next to the trainmaster's office—and you'll be furnished a brakeman's equipment. Good luck, kid."

The so-called "passport" Casey discovered was a notification to freight conductors that he was starting out to learn the road, and directing that he be shown consideration and given a helping hand. It bore the signature of the superintendent and had been written by his own hand.

At last he was a regular Railroad Man. Soon he would find a place in a locomotive cab.

Much to Casey's delight, his first call was to accompany Bose Lashley's northbound train back to Columbus, with the understanding that he would probably be sent from there southward again as far as Whistler —virtually the entire length of the road at that time.

A switch engine helper stood conveniently on the next siding, prepared to close in behind the heavy freight and lend its additional power up the heavy grade northward out of the Jackson yards.

The M. & O. entered the town from the northwest, the yards being eastward from the business center; and the Illinois Central, represented by the northeast-southwest line of the letter X already referred to, descended a steep grade into the Chester Street yards. Still farther southward, the I. C. soon was to establish another extensive yard to be known as Frogmoor. A rapidly growing volume of traffic constantly overflowing from Chester Street yard made this extension necessary.

But there was a fly in the ointment of his pleasure over this first trip as a railroad man. Although he had loitered at the boarding house as long as he could that morning, he had failed to catch a glimpse of the beauteous Jane Brady.

The trip north was so uneventful that only one detail of it was implanted in Casey's memory. He was disappointed that he should be carried through Cayce after nightfall, his old friends thus being deprived of the pleasure of recognizing him nonchalantly balancing atop a high car, his shiny new lantern swinging from the crook of an arm.

Southbound again the next day, and again with Bose Lashley. All train crews were working long shifts. Casey was turned over to the tender ministrations of Bob Sawyer, head shack on this particular southbound trip. Sawyer's acknowledgement of the introduction was not encouraging. His eye ran over Casey's elongated form and he said gruffly:

"You're a hell of a big fella, but do you know anything?"

"Yeh," the boy retorted. "Everything from dispatching trains to winding the brake wheel on a car till the wheels slide. What you want me to tell you?"

Bob Sawyer's face broke into a grin.

"Telegraph operator, hey? What a lot of use you'll be to this train's crew. If you're so wise, tell me this: what's the last thing we do before we pull out?"

"Old timer," responded Casey, returning the friendly grin, "you take one side of the train and I'll take the other. Check up on all car doors; make sure they're fastened. Rustle all the coupling pins and broken links we can find because we'll need 'em to take up slack in the couplings. If we can't find pins and links laying 'round, we'll snitch 'em from some of these strings of cars standing on the sidings."

"Fella," said Bob Sawyer heartily, "you'll do. You're born to be a gen-u-ine rail."

"Me?" said Casey loftily. "Why, me, I'm going to be a hoghead driving this or some railroad's crack trains while you're still rustling links and pins."

"Hate yourself, don't you?" said Bob Sawyer.

"Nix. I just *know* what I'm headed for." Casey confidently assured him.

CHAPTER XIV

RETRIBUTION

W HEN the conductor, Elliott, showed up carrying a set of orders, Bose Lashley read them aloud to the conductor—observance of a strict rule. Casey pictured himself doing the same thing at no distant date.

He was aware that the head brakeman, Bob Sawyer, was keeping an eye on him, being only too eager to make some caustic comment if he did anything out of order.

Casey knew that when they started, the main line switch would have to be thrown over to let the train out upon the main track. This he did without being told. As the train crawled past, he caught the fourth car from the engine and impudently thumbed his nose at the alert Sawyer. He watched for a signal from the caboose that the train had cleared and that the switch was once more closed and locked—a signal which he relayed to Bose Lashley in the engine cab.

They were on their way. No veteran rail could have expedited the start in better form.

Casey Jones was still just a youngster, but as his determination was set upon becoming a locomotive engineer, likewise had he resolved some day to marry

Jane Brady.   Nothing ever swerved him from these
two resolutions.

During the succeeding days Casey was afforded little
enough time to brood over what he was pleased to call
his troubles.   The annual grain rush was on in earnest
and it was no uncommon thing for train and engine
crews to work thirty-six hours on a stretch.   As soon
as he pulled into Jackson, as likely as not he would be
called to take a run to Okolona, Mississippi, then to
Meridian and thence to Mobile.   There might be a
few hours of sleep snatched at each point, but at best
it was a hard, grueling grind and only the boy's superb
physique enabled him to carry on without sinking from
fatigue.

And on whichever end of the line he worked he
knew eventually it would bring him back to Jackson,
where he and Jane Brady could exchange a few shy
words of conversation, timidly gaze at one another and
separate in a few minutes without either of them uttering one sane syllable.   Those brief minutes with
her did more than anything else to sustain him on the
long tiring runs.   He had found an incentive that
made him more determined than ever to find the
coveted place in the engine cab on which his heart was
set.

Although the boy Casey Jones was acquiring many
hardening bumps and mishaps, he had learned to take
it, as one might say today, on the chin and with a grin.
And furthermore he revealed at times a surprising

streak of sentiment which testified to the inherent fineness of the man as long as he lived.

For instance, he had been settled at Mrs. Brady's boarding house at Jackson long enough to be regarded as a permanent fixture—if a railroad man located at a central division point and subjected to call at any time to run either direction can be said to have any permanency. During one of his layover periods at Jackson, without mentioning the matter to Bose or anyone else, he went to the cemetery where Steve Gowdy was buried and hunted up his old friend's grave. It was with a sense of shock that he discovered the spot to be overrun with briars and weeds and no marker to designate his old friend's last resting place.

Casey hunted up the sexton, obtained scythe, hoe and other necessary tools, and when he left the cemetery at sundown no plot in the place presented a neater or more attractive appearance than the one where Steve lay. A few days later a small, plain but appropriate granite stone was to be found at the head of Steve Gowdy's grave. As long as Casey lived the plot never again presented a neglected appearance.

His occasional overnight layovers at Columbus had a curious feature. He had not been braking for many months but it seemed to him that years had elapsed since he was associated with C-Y yard offices. Lem Miller, the agent, seemed years older. Cunny did not impress him with the weight of authority that he had in the past. Indeed, the operator was a trifle shy in the presence of the one time callow student and appeared disposed to defer to his opinions, as if they bore more weight than they had in the past. He treated Casey with a degree of respect that secretly irked the huge boy.

"Cunny," he bluntly accosted his friend one night, "do you think you'll ever amount to anything?"

Taken aback, Cunny could only stutter his surprise.

"Why—why—I—I—whatcha mean?"

"I mean you're a damn' fool to keep pluggin' along here, like old Lem. Now take this fella they've sent here to take Charley Spencer's place. I been watching him. You've forgot more about railroading than he'll ever learn, yet he's the pushin', persistent kind that's goin' to keep climbin' toward the top. I bet he ain't at C-Y six months."

Cunny was glad of an opportunity to change the subject. This sort of frank talk was embarrassing.

"Speaking of Spencer," he said with a grin, "I got something for you. Wait a minute." Cunny dived into the freight house and reappeared in a moment bearing Casey's battered old patent-leather valise. He explained:

"Sent it last week from St. Louis with a note thanking you. Says he had a good job in the Illinois Central offices but expects soon to be transferred to New Orleans."

Casey, tickled to recover the old heirloom, contemplated it fondly.

"Now there you are," he said in a moment. "Take Charley Spencer; we all felt sorry for him; but what does he do? Cuts every tie behind him, burns his bridges, clutches destiny by the throat, as Pa would say, and gets something worthwhile—takes his girl right from her parents and lands in a topnotch job. You'll see Charley Spencer goin' places."

Cunny grew a bit resentful under the erstwhile student's caustic remarks and superior manner. He was emboldened to say:

"I don't see that you've gone so far. Still flippin' the rear end of freight trains."

"Tut, my boy," returned Casey, "you don't know what you're talking about. Within thirty days you'll see Casey Jones knocking on a firebox door."

"What makes you so sure?"

"Last layover at Jackson I went to the Major and told him that I knew the road, Columbus to Whistler, as well as his oldest rail. I pointed out that I'd twisted off half the brake wheels on his rolling freight stock and if he wanted to save the rest he'd better find me a berth in an engine cab. I wound up by gently reminding him there were plenty railroads that could use a husky young fireman if the M. & O. couldn't."

"You got a lot of gall. How come he didn't chase you out of his office?"

"Because he knows the muscles that can wreck brake wheels can bail tons of black diamonds where other fire-boys are shoveling only pounds. Because he knows, too, those muscles are backed by brains. Because he knows I'm a natural born railroader and that some day I'm goin' to be engineer on a crack passenger run. Get the point, Cunny. You're qualified right now to dispatch trains on the Jackson division. Go after the job."

There followed an interim during which Casey covered the entire trunkline on a sequence of runs, from Columbus to Whistler, which latter point is where the Mobile yards are located a few miles north of the city. One night he arrived back at Columbus as head shack on Bose Lashley's drag. The engineer, too, had put in long hours of continuous service and was so weary he could hardly keep awake. Casey, on the other hand, appeared to be as fresh as a daisy.

"Boy," the engineer marveled, "don't you ever get tired?"

"Nope," Casey bragged, grinning cheerfully. "Never tired of work. But looky, Bose—what's been happening? Looks like they're taking the old town apart. Wait till we cut the old mudhen loose and stable her and I'll go with you to C-Y while you register in. I talked to Cunny while we were waiting at Crockett for No. 3; he ought to be waiting for me, the bum. We'll find out whether it's a cyclone or an explosion."

The cause of this comment was the general appearance of emptiness along the right of way where the dives once flourished. Most of the buildings had vanished, an air of quiet pervaded the place. Even the brick where once Sadie Carlisle held forth was dark; even in Red Donlin's there was no light.

A few minutes later Casey was addressing Cunny while Bose Lashley stood by, an interested listener. Casey inquired:

"The Reverend Honeycutt finally blew the place up?"

"Nope," returned Cunny. "It's a funny thing. You remember the two reports Miller had me send in the day after you nearly got shot? Well, as a result the engineering department sent along a corps of surveyors and they found that all those joints, except the red brick are on the company's right of way. The chippies and their lovers were ordered out and the work of tearing down the dumps began. They made a good job of it."

"But what about Red Donlin and Sadie Carlisle?" Casey was curious to learn.

"Ah," said Cunny with a solemn air. "That's another story. You know, fella, when that guy Saunders had the fight with Mont Savage it changed her a lot. She got rid of all her girls, closed her dump, and got to taking long horseback rides into the country on a swell chestnut mare folks say Colonel Mose Terris gave her. I don't know about that. But next thing we know the Silver King is closed too. The surveyors learned that she owns the property where the brick stands as well as the Silver King property. That girl is worth a barrel of money. Next thing Saunders is found murdered on her stairway. She chases out Donlin and closes the saloon and she and that little blue-gum Guinea nigger take the body down to Saunders' old home place, near Water Valley, Mississippi. What's become of them I don't know."

Here Bose Lashley quietly spoke up.

"I can answer that. She saw that Saunders was buried in the old Saunders burying ground, then she went to her room at the hotel and put a bullet through her brain."

Casey was horrified.

"Good God! It was me gave her that pistol!"

B. H (Bose) Lashley

A portrait of the man who bestowed upon John Luther Jones the
nickname "Casey." In the early '80's Mr Lashley was an engineer on the M. & O. Later he ran an engine on the I. C.

CHAPTER XV

THE "BLUE GOOSE"

O F COURSE Casey had to explain why he had possession of the weapon and how Sadie had come to him and asked that it be returned to her. "I ought to have thrown the damn' thing into the river," he declared, and then eased his conscience with the reflection: "But I reckon she'd of died anyhow, having her mind set on it." He wondered what had become of Wallace but knew there was no use asking; nobody ever knew where a nigger disappeared to.

An interval of silence followed, the trio evidently pondering the wreckage of two misspent lives, then the boy spoke in a tone of utter weariness that was in sharp contrast with his jaunty bearing up to this moment.

"Fellas," he said, "I'm tired. Dead tired. My name ain't going to be up on the call-board tonight. And neither is yours, Bose."

"What you aiming to do?" the engineer was curious to know.

Casey hesitated. He was glad they were outside in the darkness, for he was sure he was blushing.

"Why," he falteringly offered, "I had a mind of deadheading back to Jackson."

"You mean to Mrs. Brady's," Bose Lashley drily

amended. "That's off the time-table. If we headed that direction they'd have us rounded up in no time and out on another run. Nix, kid. I got a better idea than that. The *Dan Abell* will be pulling out for Cairo shortly with the drag we just brought in. I can deadhead us up and back on her without asking for a pass. What say we ride up where I can show you the biggest railroad yards you ever dreamed of?"

Casey's memory shot back to that first evening at dusk when he stood on the river bank at Bird's Point, completely spellbound by the strange sounds that had come to him across the stream.

"We can sleep going up," Bose added, "and stay on the boat as long as we want, if we want to sleep all night. What say, Cunny? Like to come along?"

But Cunny's was not an adventurous spirit.

"No thanks," he declined. "I'd rather be at home in my own little bed. This is going to be a cold night."

The engineer's proposal appealed to Casey, who realized the impracticability of making the long journey back to Jackson that night.

"By golly, Bose, that would be something!" he assented.

The train-carrying ferry was a huge side-wheeler, open from bow to stern, like a tunnel, so that strings of cars might be run on at one end and off at the other. There were no accommodations for passengers, but the officers and crew had comfortable quarters and there were any number of warm nooks where trainmen, evidently stealing away from the call-board even as Lashley and Casey Jones were doing, could curl up and snooze in undisturbed quiet. This seemed to be a common thing on the big river railroad ferries. And in almost no time at all our adventurers, spent with fatigue, were lost to the world. Nor did anybody awaken them when the boat drew into the slip at Cairo and its cargo of freight cars was run off to the shore tracks.

Indeed the hour was well along toward dawn when finally they bestirred themselves and, much refreshed, disembarked.

The whole thing gave the boy an almost continuous thrill. The darkness was filled with sounds, most of them familiar, some distant, some nearer at hand, but all having one source—the railroad. Out of this seeming confusion had arisen the enchantment that had enthralled him years ago when he stood upon the river bank at Bird's Point.

The spark-like gleam of lard oil lanterns bobbed here and there, describing circles, half-circles, spasmodical, vertical jerks, each motion a signal to an unseen engineer. Yellow head-light beams, gigantic lances of light, stabbed the darkness; some moving forward or backward, others stationary. Gently hissing steam denoted locomotives at rest, waiting in readiness to go; heavy rumbling wheels, the dull, weighty metallic clank and clatter of loose rod bearings, noticeable while an engine was drifting, and the explosive bursting roar of pop-valves, were indications that many other locomotives were exceedingly busy about their affairs.

Oddly, Casey at once sensed something unfamiliar about the place.

"Where are we?" he abruptly asked Bose Lashley.

"We are," his companion informed him "up to our necks in the Illinois Central yards at Cairo. And it's some place."

"Ah-ha!" Casey jubilated. "I thought so. There's something different about the very air."

It was still too dark to view much of the extensive yards, but the boy knew that there must be miles upon miles of tracks hidden under the cloak of night. A tangy smell of the river was noticeable. Frequently the hoarse bellow of a steamboat whistle mingled with the other sounds. A delicious odor compounded of coal smoke, steam and hot oil tingled the nostrils. Altogether Casey was kept keyed up to a high pitch of thoroughly enjoyable excitement, immersed in a spell that he had no inclination to break by talking.

So this was what the eddying river mists had veiled from his boyish eyes that memorable night so long ago!

To Bose Lashley it was, however, an old story; his thoughts were just now occupied by more practicable matters.

"Say, you long-legged galliwumpus," he suddenly burst forth, "don't you ever get hungry?"

"Now that you've mentioned it," Casey confessed,

"I do. I am. But where does a fella eat in a place like this? It must be miles to the nearest greasy spoon."

"Here's where you learn something, Bud. Stick close to papa and get acquainted with the Blue Goose— the only eating-joint I know of that sits in the center of a busy railroad yard. We both need a man's size serving of that good old reliable standby, Trainman's Delight."

"Meaning which?"

"T-bone steak, french fried potatoes, and cream gravy."

The Blue Goose was an institution of the good old days known to trainmen from Kansas City, St. Louis, Chicago, Pittsburgh and points between to the Gulf of Mexico. At one time or another they inevitably gravitated to this distinctively trainmen's restaurant. Its presiding genius was Jimmy Dinsmore and his familiar greeting of "Name it, boys—I got it" was equivalent to uttering the passwords to a secret order. It mattered not that Jimmy usually was unable to produce any desired delicacies outside of the restricted and conventional bill of fare, but he could supply a substitute guaranteed to be equally as good and satisfying.

The long counter with its row of high stools in front, its clusters of heavy china sugar-bowls and condiment jars and bottles, its enormous glass bells inverted over cakes, ready-made sandwiches and like delicacies, its greasy fly netting shielding baked hams stuck full of cloves, roasts of beef and pork and rows of pastry—all

of these Jimmy Dinsmore presided over and passed out
to the hungry rails, along with steaming coffee in cups
so heavy that they would have broken one's foot if ever
allowed to fall upon it.

The Blue Goose was famous for its pies, both open-
face and hunting-case models, its oyster stews and, par
excellence, its T-bone steaks, smoking from the broiler
grill and swimming in a delectable admixture of their
own juices and melted butter.

In a big busy railroad yard no hour is quieter than
another, and now, close on to daybreak, a sound of
many voices inside the restaurant indicated that it was
doing a thriving business.

The step Casey Jones took in the wake of Bose
Lashley that carried him across the threshold of the
Blue Goose was one of the most fateful of his entire
career.

CHAPTER XVI

BOOMER BILL DRISCOLL

AMID the hubbub of voices a sentence or a phrase
now and then stood out distinctly. At first it was
all very confusing to the young giant from the Mobile
& Ohio, but in a moment what he heard gave him one
thrill after another.

". . . you louse! You know damn well, Spike, it
was on the Denver & Rio Grande. . . . Well, well,
well! You old Lackawanna spooner! When did you
blow in? . . . No sir, I tell you it was two year ago
come December I seen you last. You was straw boss at
Winnemucca on the U-P, an' I was firin' for old man
Hodges" . . . "Baltimore & Ohio" . . . "down on
the Katy" . . . "be back on the Aransas Pass in less'n
a week" . . . and so on and on and on. The clamor
was deafening.

But to the ears of Casey, who had never been anywhere away from the M. & O. trunkline, the names of
distant railroads and far away places were as sweet
music. These rough, coarse voiced fellows had been
everywhere, seen everything. They were hard-
featured, hard-fisted, not knowing what it meant to
knuckle down to any man.

Bose Lashley's voice broke into his absorption.

131

"Look 'em over, Casey. Here you see in one big noisy herd that strange product of the railroad known as the Boomer Railroader. Floaters who can't stick anywhere. Jump from one road to another, usually clear across the country. Never so happy as when they quit one job and ride the rods or blind baggage somewhere else to find another just like the one they left. It's the grain rush that's started them drifting through St. Louis. They know there'll be plenty of work with good pay while the grain is moving."

Casey's attention suddenly was drawn to a huge, hulking fellow wearing a high-peaked wool cap, high arctic overshoes buckled over the lower part of his baggy, dirty trousers. He slouched up with a bear-like movement and held out a grimy paw. His hoarse voice bellowed in an attempt at joviality:

"If it ain't Bose Lashley, strike me dead! Bose, you old hell-driving hoghead, how are you?"

Bose failed to warm to this boisterous greeting. The other appeared to be thunderstruck.

"Good God'll mighty!" he yelled. "You ain't forgot Bill Driscoll, have you?"

Bose slowly shook his head.

"No," he responded, "I haven't forgot you."

The extended paw, unnoticed, sank slowly.

An ugly look appeared upon Bill Driscoll's face, which was sorely in need of a shave. His lips curled back, and Casey marveled that a human could possess a

mouthful of such black and broken teeth.   The fellow
snarled:

"By God, you're just as stuck up as ever, ain't you?
You need to have your head beat off."

Bose did not flinch, nor did his level regard swerve
from the coarse visage before him.   Then quite suddenly it was borne in upon Casey that everybody present
was afraid of this huge bully, who undoubtedly could
have killed the slighter built Bose with his bare hands,
and that in case of a clash, which seemed imminent, no
one would intervene to help the engineer.   Casey was
ever slow to anger, but all at once he saw red.   Instinctively he caught Bill Driscoll by the nearest shoulder and spun him round.   As a matter of fact, so much
power was put into the spinning operation that Driscoll
lost his balance and staggered backward.

Instantly Driscoll recovered and switched his attention to Casey.

"Why, you young punk!" he sputtered his astonishment.   "I'll tear your head off!".

Casey retorted in a tone that was deceptively quiet:

"Fella, you were addressing a gentleman.   Apolo-
gize or you'll take a licking."

With a roar Driscoll plunged at him.

What followed was Homeric, though so soon over.
Casey's long left arm shot out mechanically to ward off
the furious onrush. His fingers twined into the red
bandanna handkerchief encircling Driscoll's neck, and

the fellow halted as abruptly as if he had collided with the end of a wooden beam. The vicious blow he had aimed at the boy fell harmlessly short.

Next, unpleasant choking noises began to burst from Bill Driscoll. His wind was shut off. He felt that it was his own head being torn loose. The red bandanna was twisted like a tourniquet until his eyes bulged and his tongue hung out. The fellow was abjectly helpless.

Casey's right arm suddenly swept round, the open palm striking the side of Driscoll's face and head with a blow that would have felled a mule. The fellow went limp, but Casey did not allow him to sink to the floor.

Instead, he jerked the half-conscious body toward himself in order to obtain leverage and momentum. Then he tossed the boomer from him with a mighty heave that sent the huge hulk of him sailing through the air. He landed among his cronies, scattering them helter-skelter. Two of them remained motionless on the floor underneath Driscoll's huddled, inert frame.

Utter silence fell. Everybody stared in amazement at this mild appearing young giant who had suddenly gone, as Jimmy Dinsmore put it, hog wild. And presently, when Boomer Bill Driscoll struggled back to consciousness and rose groggily to his feet, none was more astonished than he. With one hand he wiped the fog from his eyes. His jaw sagged as he gaped dazedly at his antagonist.

Driscoll lurched toward Casey. Coming to a halt at

a safe distance from those deadly long arms, he addressed the boy:

"Fella, nobody ever done that to me before. I didn't think any man living could. But don't forget this: some day I'll get you and when I do it'll be just too bad for you."

By this time Casey was more disgusted with the man than angered at him. In reply he raised a potent fist and moved forward a step. In tones still quiet but carrying a deadly intent, he said:

"You lousy bum. Are you beggin' to be murdered? If you ain't, get out o' here and stay out as long as I and my friend are here."

Driscoll hesitated but a moment, then turned and walked quickly from the Blue Goose. And excepting as Boomer Bill Driscoll lingers in song and legend, he passes from the pages of this chronicle.

The ovation now showered upon Casey Jones quite overwhelmed him with embarrassment. He did not know what to say to this crowd of rails who seemed intent upon making a hero of him.

Casey was entirely ignorant of Driscoll's evil reputation. The big boomer had bullied his way along the railroad lines for years, striking terror to the hearts of the weak and timid and being shunned as a dangerous animal by the more courageous but less stout of muscle than he.

Especially was this true respecting the Negroes. With them he was cruelly overbearing and it was said that he had killed more than one for sheer lust of slaughter.

An alert, bright-eyed, firm-jawed young fellow in overalls and jumper now pushed to the front of the press surrounding Casey and found a place beside Lashley. No one could have mistaken his calling; tallowpot was written all over him.

"I came in at the start of the fracas," announced he, "and I want to say no words of mine could do it justice. Boy, what a beautiful ruckus! Bose, I'd be proud to meet this husky young friend of yours."

Lashley gave the young fellow a friendly glance.

"Sure," he responded. "Casey Jones, shake hands with Lee Chandler."

Thus did Casey meet the first of the quartet of Chandler brothers.

CHAPTER XVII

THE WORK SONG

CASEY JONES was a young giant, standing six feet four without his shoes. He came rightly by his extraordinary size and strength, for his father was six feet four; each of his brothers stood above six feet; his mother and sister likewise were unusually tall. The full extent of sheer physical strength that he possessed he himself never suspected until his encounter with Bill Driscoll. It was this strapping youth who so favorably impressed Major Hosford that ironclad regulations regarding age limitations were abrogated in order that he might not have to wait to embark upon his career of railroad man.

The almost immediate results of his combat with Driscoll were wholly unexpected. The boomer had lorded it so long all up and down the trunklines where he had found employment that news of his downfall at the hands of a mere stripling was received with incredulity.

Who was this Casey Jones who had so handily brought about the bully's undoing?

As news of the exploit traveled, it was enlarged and embroidered and decorated with imaginative touches until it became a glamourous St. George and the Dragon or a David and Goliath sort of feat.

It was some time, however, before Casey became aware of the widespread glorification of his conquest of Bill Driscoll. The deed had been accomplished with as much ease as if the big bully had been merely a bad little boy courting punishment, and although temporarily gratified by the excitement and adulation of the moment, the realistic young rail could not be expected to attach any lasting importance to the incident. But railroaders over the country were beginning to regard the name Casey Jones as that of a hero, and finally one night during the summer following the downfall of Driscoll the personal significance of the Blue Goose episode was brought home to Casey under colorful and dramatic circumstances.

As opportunity arose, when he was on Bose Lashley's run into Columbus, the pair would board one or another of the huge railroad ferries and enjoy the restful ride to Cairo and back. The multitudinous things the railroad had to offer at Cairo never ceased to be a source of wonder to Casey.

One night the two young rails were watching a gang of Negro workmen unload some pieces of heavy machinery on the Cairo waterfront. The boys labored in the red glow of smoking, flaring torches, presenting a weird and interesting picture.

But what arrested the two friends was the song the laborers were chanting while they worked.

"Lift 'em up—lay 'em down——
Lift 'em up—lay 'em down——"

The chant came in unison from the throats, marking time for a similar perfect unison of muscular effort expended, which caused Casey to remark:

"If darkies didn't sing while they work they would get mighty little done."

The song went on.

"Lift 'em up—lay 'em down——
Boomer Bill has come to town."

From Casey bubbled a subdued laugh. "It's about Boomer Bill!" exclaimed he.

"Clar de track fo' Boomer Bill!
He's big an' tough an' hahd to kill!

Lift 'em up—lay 'em down!"

Lashley's interest was mounting, too, by this time. "Listen!" he murmured.

But Casey needed no urging to listen. He was straining his ears not to miss a word of the work song.

"Black man, dis ain't no time fo' to play——
Boomer Bill git you ef you loafs dat way.

Lift 'em up—lay 'em down——
Boomer Bill has come to town!"

What came next electrified both listeners.

"Boomer Bill come rarin' at Casey Jones
  Fo' to eat him up an' scrunch his bones——"

"You hear that?" suddenly cried Casey. "You hear
'em singing 'bout me?"
  "Shut up!" snapped Bose.

"Casey cotch Bill wid his big lef' hand——
    Lift 'em up—lay 'em down!
  An he fling Boomer Bill to the Promis' Land
    Lift 'em up—lay 'em down——
  Boomer Bill has come to town!

  Boomer Bill light on the Golden Shoah——
  Boomer Bill ain't comin' back no mo'——
    Lift 'em up—lay 'em down!"

This was too much. With one accord Bose and
Casey scrambled together down the clay bank and spoke
to the gang's colored boss.
  "Boy," Bose demanded, "where did you learn that
song? Where did it come from?"
  The boy's face lighted up; he was tremendously
pleased by this notice.
  "You mean dat Boomer Bill song? Wh', Cap'n, suh,
hit's a song fum de Black Riveh country. Niggehs say
a niggeh cunjur man down dere made dat song."
  Casey's interest quickened. He suddenly asked:

"You know his name?"

One of the work gang spoke up.

"I knows him boss. He's a runty little Guinea niggeh whut wuks in de roundhouse at Canton. Folks calls him Wallace."

Bose grinned knowingly.

The information confirmed Casey's quick suspicion as to the origin of the song, but left him wondering. Why should he, Casey Jones, become prominent and his name featured in a song simply because he had put a bragging bully in his proper place?—Well, anyhow it wasn't exactly unpleasant to be popular all up and down the Valley, even if it didn't make sense!

When he returned to Jackson and Mrs. Brady's boarding house he was emboldened to seek out Jane Brady and tell her about the work song—one of the few occasions of his early courtship when he could muster up courage to address her. And he was gratified when he saw that she was properly impressed.

"It is indeed strange," she said, "you see what a hero you are."

"Aw, shucks!" stammered Casey, coloring to the roots of his hair. Nor could he think of anything else to say until Miss Brady departed to resume her neglected household duties.

CHAPTER XVIII

LOYALTY

THE halo that encircled Casey's head as a result of his encounter with Boomer Bill Driscoll was having its repercussions. The work song was only one manifestation. Frequently, in mingling with his associates, Casey found that he was treated with what seemed an exaggerated respect. He was rapidly learning that fame carries certain marked disadvantages.

However, the homage did tickle his vanity; he admitted this in later years to friends and contemporaries who had bestowed upon him an accolade for accomplishments much more important and significant than the conquest of Boomer Bill—accomplishments pertaining to his life work which remain important factors to this day.

Strutting with becoming modesty in the bright light that shines upon the hero, he had argued himself into a conviction that Jane Brady would consent to marry him if he could screw up courage to ask her. He had almost whipped himself into this state of mind when he received a message from his father stating that he was sorely in need of additional financial assistance. The pedagogue, in anticipation of being transferred to the school at Jordan, some four miles from Cayce, had obligated himself to buy a home. Could Casey contribute one-half his monthly earnings and support himself comfortably on the balance?

Casey could. But to do so would mean that he would have to postpone the proposal to Jane until he began earning more money. In other words, until he arrived at the righthand side of a locomotive cab.

Then came his next big opportunity, even before he expected it. And it came about because, even as he owed his first connection with the railroad to the fact that he was a good baseball player, now he was recognized as a proficient telegraph operator.

"Casey, you've wanted to get in an engine cab for some time. Is that still your ambition?"

"Sure is, Major Hosford. If anything, more than ever."

"All right. Tomorrow report to Engineer Sam Merritt, engineer of a work train operating out of Whistler. Of course a work train is something different from a train running on regular schedule. You know it usually operates under general orders and has to accommodate itself to everything else traveling over the main line. My boy, you will divide your time between firing for Sam Merritt and acting as emergency operator, keeping in touch with your dispatcher. Here is the order to Sam Merritt, and here is a pass that will deadhead you to Whistler on any train. Good luck."

Again the boy was jubilant. So his braking days were over and he had gained a foothold in an engine cab. He had to hurry to Mrs. Brady's and tell Jane about it. She congratulated him and expressed pleasure over the change in his fortunes in a manner so quiet that it dampened his ardor.

"Aren't you really glad, Jane—er—Miss Brady?"

"Of course I'm glad for you." She pondered, then asked: "How long will you have to fire before you will be promoted to an engineer's job? Four years, isn't it?"

Had he been keen enough he would have detected that these questions gave a hint at the reason for her lack of enthusiasm.

"Four years?" he repeated. "What's four years? With more pay I can really begin savin' money—even though I keep on sendin' my father half of it."

The lovely gray eyes gave him a long speculative look.

"Casey Jones," she said in a moment, "that responsibility is unfair to you. The idea of sending your father half your pay twice a month!"

She hurried from the room.

There were two details in her last remark that made him think. Just what did she mean by so warmly denying that he owed this responsibility to his parents? And it was the first time she had ever called him Casey. True, she had lent it a formality by including his full name, Casey Jones, but still the sound of Casey on her lips was pleasant.

No wonder the boy was worried. He embarked for Whistler that night, his heart aching with love for her, every fiber of his being yearning to have her for his very own.

CHAPTER XIX

THE WORK TRAIN

CASEY, in his newest and nattiest suit, boarded No. 1, fast southbound express, and found himself a seat in the chair car where he could utilize the old patent-leather valise as a pillow when it was not reposing in the metal rack overhead. He soon lapsed into deep sleep, dreaming of Jane and hoping that this new tide in his fortunes would enable them to unite their destinies.

His dream was shattered when the chime of the engine whistle was flung back along the train: a sustained mellow note indicating the approach to a station.

Whistler.

The train slipped slowly through the extensive railroad yards, lighted only occasionally by oil headlights, the spark-gleam of lard oil lanterns in the hands of busy switchmen, and now and then a flaring kerosene torch.

The "brains," as the conductor was known in the vernacular, thrust his head in at the car door to make the station call in a gruff baritone voice.

"Whistler! Whistler! This way out."

Then to the still drowsy dead-head, "Persons, our hoghead, says you're Casey Jones."

146

"Yeh," Casey returned, sitting upright and stretching himself. "What about it?"

"Fella, wish I'd known it when you got aboard. You'd had better sleeping quarters. But we got no time to get better acquainted now. You got to light here if you want the Whistler roundhouse. That's it where you see that flock of gas lights. We're moving slow enough for you to hop off. See you later."

Casey found the night foreman still on duty.

"I'm Casey Jones," he began, but was not allowed to finish. The foreman was exceedingly warm in his welcoming of the newcomer.

"So you're the fella that licked Boomer Bill Driscoll," said he admiringly. "Set yourself in this chair. Smoke a seegar? No? Well, I ain't got nothing but water to drink till we can get together later." He pawed out a yellow sheet from among the litter on his desk and passed it to Casey with the explanation: "This is what the boss got from the master mechanic."

Casey read:

"Am sending Fireman J. L. Jones with instructions to report to you. He is learning road as fireman. Is experienced telegraph operator-brakeman and will serve purpose as first-class fireman."

"How should I know," the foreman said, "that J. L. Jones and Casey Jones are one and the same?"

"What do I do next?" Casey wanted to know.

"Just report on call, to engineer Sam Merritt. You'll find yourself in a soft job on a work-train-extra leaving here in the morning to put in an indefinite time up around Vinegar Bend, Escatawpa and Citronelle. The work train needs a smart rail like you who can pound the key as well as keep the kettle's kite flying. You'll like Sam Merritt."

Sam Merritt dated back to the old wood burning days and cabbage head stacks that showered sparks generously over a wide stretch of countryside adjacent to the right of way, providing the company's adjuster with innumerable claims arising from fires. No student fireman could have had a better tutor than Sam Merritt, a good-natured hoghead who took a shine to the lad at once and—much to Casey's relief—did not refer to Boomer Bill Driscoll.

Some brief consideration is given to the four weeks that Casey Jones spent with the work-train-extra operating out of Whistler for several important reasons.

In the first place, it may be considered the culminating point of the formative period of Casey's life. In the next place, as a step leading to the completeness of his knowledge and experience, the informality of the work train afforded him opportunities to operate the engine, which was the fulfillment of a dream. Then, too, the prolonged absence from Jane Brady grew so intolerable that he determined to make her his wife, regardless of financial conditions. And finally, it was during this period that Casey made up his mind that some day he would be baptized. Jane was a Roman Catholic; and Casey, without conviction, decided that he would identify himself with that religious sect in order to strengthen his suit.

Once clear of the Whistler yards, the work-train-extra was pretty much of a law unto itself, as far as the train crew were concerned. Bill Morris, gang foreman, and his straw boss, one Narcisse Germain, had a definite program of work to be done with a large gang of Negro laborers.

The very first day out Casey encountered something that gave him a queer feeling. Through the medium of some mysterious grapevine agency, the gang of black-birds—numbering nearly a hundred—learned his identity. He found himself, accordingly, an object of deference which amounted in some instances to almost worshipful attention. On one or two occasions this worked out with tremendous benefit to him. Whenever trouble arose among the blacks which the gang foreman or straw boss could not immediately iron out with their bluster and blasphemies, Casey could settle with a quiet word, and the small army of darkies would become entirely tractable.

Oak Grove was the first stop, where three cars of steel were picked up and added to the train. Then, at Yellow Pine, a general unloading was effected, for at this point cross-ties and steel were dumped upon the right of way and the work of laying a temporary spur was begun. The purpose of the spur was to accommodate the camp and work cars, keeping the main line and the regular passing-track clear.

When the work of spiking rails commenced, Casey's attention was drawn to a black giant who answered to the name of Hambone. The labor of lifting and carrying and placing the steel had to be performed in unison, and Hambone proved to be the song leader of the parts of the gang thus engaged.

> "Lift 'em up—lay 'em down——
> Boomer Bill has come to town!"

Sam Merritt, lolling back on his leather cushion in the motionless locomotive, looked across at a surprised fireboy and snickered. He said:

"You young squirt, you'll never live long enough to live that down."

"Hell!" said Casey disgustedly.

CHAPTER XX

THE CHALLENGE

THE main function of the work-train-extra was shifting the work gang from point to point to transfer and unload carloads of ballast and steel. At times when operations blocked the main line, brakemen were kept stationed the regulation distance—99 telegraph poles—both directions from where the work was in progress, their purpose being to flag approaching trains.

The work train had not been shuttling back and forth many days when Sam Merritt proposed that Casey try his hand at operating the engine, and within a few minutes the old hoghead realized that this big, ambitious, good-natured boy could handle a locomotive as well as he himself, and with a sort of natural aptitude that was amazing.

Following this incident, when there was much shunting of cars to be done, or a run to be made north of Yellow Pine for a fresh cargo of ballast, or perhaps a run down to Whistler for coal and water and other supplies, it was the customary practice for Merritt to exchange places with Casey, good-humoredly boasting of his own superiority as fireman. Leaving the firebox door on the latch, ready to be kicked open after the scoop was filled, he would call Casey's attention to the deftness with which he could swing the scoopful from the pile and spread the coal evenly over the fire, all in one continuous movement. No wasted effort. The boy learned something new.

This was all very gratifying to Casey; but to a young man so madly in love, four weeks was a long, long time to be separated from his beloved. In the still of the night, lying in his bunk above a blissfully snoring Sam Merritt, he confided to the darkness, "I'm going to get me back to Jackson and marry Jane, come hell or high water."

But eventful days were to elapse before this came about.

In 1882 the Mobile & Ohio was extended north from Columbus to East Cairo, Kentucky. Columbus was no longer a terminal.

After four weeks with the work-train-extra, Casey was ordered to report to the master mechanic at Jackson, where he was ordered out northward to "learn the road" as fireman.

His reunion with Jane was brief but the unmistakable joy she was unable to conceal at seeing him again sent the boy's spirits soaring.

"When I get back from this run I got something mighty important to say to you," he confided.

She returned demurely: "I hope I can find time to listen."

"You will," he called back confidently, hurrying

LEE CHANDLER

Portrait of Illinois Central engineer who was a close friend of
Casey Jones and played an important part in his career.

away to catch Bill Flickenger on the north run to East Cairo.

There was a night's layover at East Cairo, then back to Jackson and out again on the north run. Between the two terminals there is a stretch of about twenty miles where the right of way of the Mobile & Ohio and the Illinois Central parallel each other scarcely a stone's throw apart.

Steaming northward at a satisfactory speed with a drag that was not particularly heavy, they had drawn close to Ft. Jefferson, now designated Winthrop, when the smoke of a northbound Illinois Central locomotive became conspicuous. Shortly the two trains were abreast. As they drew closer Casey recognized the man at the throttle of the Illinois Central hog. It was Lee Chandler.

Gradually Chandler drew ahead of Flickenger. Casey glanced at the steam gage and saw that his engine was carrying a full head. Nevertheless he banged open the firebox door and spread a couple of scoopfuls of coal over an already satisfactory fire.

At the point where the two right of ways were closest Lee Chandler leaned from his cab window and, with a thumb against his nose, wiggled the fingers in a gesture that was conspicuously derisive and, to Casey, humiliating. He called across to Bill Flickenger:

"You goin' to let him run away from us like that?"

"Boy," returned Bill unemotionally, "we're doing all we dast now."

Casey stared at his engineer, a man he once had deemed a sort of demigod. Never again did he know the feeling of veneration for Bill Flickenger he had harbored in earlier years.

What would Bose Lashley have done had he been in Bill Flickenger's place? Bose Lashley, the engineer who always ran slambang past the Water Tank at Cayce?

Casey got the answer to this a few days later when he went north out of Jackson to East Cairo on a run that brought them and Lee Chandler's train into Ft. Jefferson at the same time.

"If Lee's not behind the advertised," Lashley called across the cab to his fireboy, "we'll be picking him up in about three minutes." Bose knew he had a good fire. He glanced at his gauges and again called across to Casey:

"Giv'er all you know how, Bud. This old kettle is foul and he may have an advantage of us there, but he'll have to make his fireboy shovel black diamonds to keep even. There he comes!"

In less than three minutes Chandler's train was abreast of theirs. He could be seen studying the situation, then he turned and said something to his fireman. Black smoke billowed from his stack and his drag slowly climbed ahead.

Lashley suddenly yelled: "Knock that firebox door!"

As though Casey was not already giving her all she could take. But he threw open the door, spread the white hot fire to an even bed and fed it four more scoopfuls of coal.

Perhaps thirty seconds of this, then Lashley, watching the right of way ahead of him and Chandler's train from a corner of his eye, said:

"Boy, it's not our fault. His hog is in better condition and his drag is lighter than ours. But he's only ahead of us by seconds."

Casey dropped upon his leather cushion, took off his cap and wiped his brow.

"But," he said dejectedly, "he's beatin' us. I don't give a damn if we never get into East Cairo."

Bose Lashley laughed.

"He'll kid us plenty when we get to the Blue Goose, but it's not our fault. He's only one up on me for I've outrun him many a time."

"Bose," said Casey solemnly, "one of these days I'm goin' to have me a hog on the I-C, and I'm goin' to make running records that even Lee Chandler can't thumb his nose at."

CHAPTER XXI

A NEW FRIEND

CASEY JONES was in a dejected frame of mind
when they pulled into East Cairo. He could not
forget Lee Chandler outrunning Bose Lashley, even
by a few seconds.

It was nightfall when their extra arrived at East
Cairo, and to forestall the possibility of a call-boy find-
ing them with orders to double back south immediately,
Lashley and Casey crossed the Ohio on the big Illinois
Central train ferry, *William H. Osborne*, and sought
the "seclusion" of the Blue Goose restaurant.

Here Casey's reception was boisterous. Jimmy Dinsmore, in addition to his familiar "Name it boys—I got
it," insisted on shaking hands and assuring Casey that
whatever he ordered tonight would be on the house.
No Boomer Bill Driscoll or other disturbing element
was present and the entire crowd showed only a disposition to gather round and enjoy themselves.

As Lee Chandler entered, he immediately espied
Lashley and the latter's fireboy. Then the ribbing
began.

"Did you have to carry that old kettle of yours in?"
he asked Lashley. "Or did you leave that chore to this
husky fireboy?"

"We're here ahead of you, ain't we?" Lashley countered.

"Huh!" Chandler grunted. "That's only because my drag had to be run on the ferry for the river crossing." His eye ran over Casey's tall muscular frame.

"Looks like a fella who can throw bums like Boomer Bill around as easy as you oughtn't to have any trouble keeping Lashley's kite flying."

Casey regarded him gloomily. Then he said:

"Chandler, I don't like to boast, but one o' these days I'll be showin' you I-C hogheads how to run an engine. You'll learn from Casey Jones how to keep ahead of the advertised."

Lee Chandler laughed. "Oh no, you don't like to boast! You just like to crow and flap your wings. Come on over, boy, whenever you're ready. The running over our way is fine."

Later in the evening Lashley and Casey were in a well known downtown resort where they found a crap game in full swing. Lashley called his companion's attention to a short, heavyset youth who was intent on "rolling the bones," but apparently without much success.

"See that youngster?" said Lashley. "That's the youngest of the Chandler quartet—Ed's and Lee's and Paul's youngest brother, Colie Chandler. He's an I-C call-boy but some day will be an engineer, just like all the Chandlers." *

* See Appendix, note 13.

Casey regarded with interest the boy who was so absorbed in the dice game.

"Folks call him Runt," Bose went on. "He has a voice you could hear across the Mississippi River."

At this moment Colie Chandler tossed his overcoat to a nearby house attendant. "Gimme a dollar on that," he loudly demanded.

Without a word the attendant tucked the coat under an arm and flipped Colie a silver dollar.

"Shoot the dollar," announced Colie.

In another minute dollar and overcoat both were gone and Colie Chandler contemplated the bystanders with undisturbed cheerfulness.

"Well," he announced, "that's one way to get me out of a crap game."

"Yeh," Bose Lashley addressed him, "and you better be getting back on your job. They don't send call-boys out after call-boys who loaf."

Colie Chandler was viewing with interest the immense frame of Casey Jones.

"Mr. Lashley," he asked respectfully, "isn't that Casey Jones?"

"Sure is, Runt," replied Lashley.

The boy revealed suddenly an engaging smile.

"Mister," he said to Casey, "I'd be right proud to shake your hand."

"Sure," Casey assented, holding out his big paw.

The two shook hands, and thus began a close and lasting friendship.

CHAPTER XXII

THE BAPTISM

SCENES and situations can shift swiftly along an extensive trunkline like that of the Mobile & Ohio Railway.

Back at Jackson again, Casey was bitterly disappointed by learning that Jane Brady was off visiting friends; and before she returned to her mother's boarding house he was ordered south. Again he heard the old refrain: "We're always needing men on the South End at this season." Thus were he and Bose Lashley separated.

But before they parted Lashley confided to his young friend:

"When we see each other again I expect Mary Ellen will be my wife."

Casey stared at the young engineer. Mary Ellen, of course, was Bose's sweetheart and she was also a chum of Jane Brady's. It never had entered the boy's head, however, that she and Bose might be contemplating matrimony, even as he was planning to marry Jane.

He impulsively wrung Lashley's hand.

"Congratulations, fella," he said earnestly. "But you haven't got anything on me. As soon as I get back from the South End, Jane and I are goin' to get married too."

This was assuming a good deal, for he had not yet proposed to Jane and there was a possibility that she entertained other plans.

In those days the freight districts were long. He found himself working consistently between Okolona, through Meridian and into Whistler—virtually to the Gulf of Mexico. Most of the time he fired for freight engineers, but more than once during this period of heavy business he found himself with Engineer Walter Persons on a passenger run.

Thus the days passed and it seemed to the boy that he would never get back to Jackson and Jane again. But he wrote to her and was overjoyed when she promptly replied to his letters in a tone that was extremely friendly. Casey had no intention of proposing to her by letter, however.

Then to Whistler one morning came Bose Lashley with his bride. Right after the reunion Casey took away his friend's breath.

"Now that you're here," he said to Lashley, "I want you and Mary Ellen to do me a favor."

"Don't make it too hard," Bose cautioned.

"Well, I hope you won't think it too much to go with me to St. Bridget's church and witness my baptism by Father O'Reilly."

And so, on November 11, 1886, as the records of St. Bridget's Parish at Whistler attest, this interesting ceremony was performed by Father P. S. O'Reilly, with Mr. and Mrs. B. H. Lashley acting as sponsors. The motive behind this step, of course, was to please Jane.

Although Casey was making definite plans to be married, there was a dissatisfaction growing in him that he could not altogether define. It pertained to his work and ambitions as a railroad man.

After the Mobile & Ohio was extended through to East Cairo, the Jackson Division, Tupelo to Columbus, was abolished and with it went his good friend Major Hosford. The Major, he learned, had become the Illinois Central agent at Jackson.

Casey Jones now realized that being a good engineer implied something more than mere ability to drive a locomotive. The experiences with Lee Chandler at Ft. Jefferson had touched off a spark that was kindling the fire of his inherent genius. A vast railroad system was like an empire, and he believed that an engineer should be able to lend something to that empire that would help it advance.

It is no disparagement of the Mobile & Ohio at this period so many years ago to disclose that Casey's awakening caused him to regard with growing interest the Illinois Central Railroad. At Jackson he fraternized more and more with I. C. rails, made the acquaintance of Ed and Paul Chandler, outstanding engineers, and saw his own brothers, Eugene and Frank and Phillip, embarking upon railroad careers with the ambition of eventually becoming engineers, an ambition they all attained.

But despite the importance of these considerations

directly affecting his own immediate future, Casey was ever mindful of what he felt to be his moral obligation to help provide for his father and mother. It was impossible to see them except on rare occasions, but he heard from them nearly every week and was assured that with his continued assistance they were getting along nicely. He also had reason to believe that the brothers were making progress in their respective careers on the railroad; but his sister caused him grave concern, especially when he learned that his mother was likewise disturbed.

Between Emma and Casey there was always that inborn attachment frequently existing between an older brother and his only sister. Notwithstanding the boy's detached and somewhat condescending manner exhibited toward Emma during their childhood days, it has been pointed out that such was his attitude toward the sex generally and was in no sense an indication of lack of affection for his sister. On the contrary, he loved her with a warm and intense devotion that endured to the very end, undiminished by long periods of separation.

Emma had now cut loose from home ties and was employed in Hayes-Brown Department Store at Jackson, Tennessee. She had grown into a strikingly pretty young woman of fine figure and dashing carriage. Possessing many fine qualities, she was a fiery, impulsive creature, and apparently lacked the finely balanced character and steadfastness of purpose that might have been expected of the daughter of Frank and Ann Nolen Jones.

At Jackson Emma traveled with a pleasure-loving company of young people, and on the few occasions that Casey saw her he earnestly remonstrated with her. But she always laughed away his fears, finishing with a big hug and kiss, and Casey would be left marveling at her flamboyant good looks, her bold flashing dark eyes under tantalizing lashes, and her high spirits. What a beautiful woman his sister was! And his fears would return only after he had left her presence.

One day while they were lunching together at the Old Southern Hotel during Emma's hour off, Casey's mind reverted to their first view of the big river back at Bird's Point and he decided to ask her if she could recall what frightened her.

"Sis, what was it threw such a scare into you that evenin' we arrived at Bird's Point? Remember?"

He saw her grow pale and a look of horror come into her fine, dark eyes. She answered him in an awed whisper.

"I saw Death, Luther,—Death in a terrible form. It —it was just as if I were about to be engulfed and destroyed!"

CHAPTER XXIII

MARRIED

THE lure of the Illinois Central grew stronger day by day, and only the thought that he would lose his seniority as fireman and might be required to embark upon another four years of apprenticeship restrained Casey Jones from making an immediate change.

Those were the days when Stuyvesant Fish and J. T. Harahan guided the destinies of that railroad. They were the men who were building it into one of the greatest systems in the world; men of vision and power who planned ahead according to potential demands and possessed the faculty of making their plans materialize.

The principal feeder lines which tapped all the grain growing territory of the Middle West at Chicago were augmented by a numerous fleet of grain bearing vessels on the Great Lakes, with the result that the amount of grain to be moved to seaboard for export was enormous. Here was where fast train operation over nearly a straight trunkline nine hundred and twelve miles south to New Orleans enabled the I. C. to secure the bulk of this rich commerce.

Fast trains meant highly skilled engineers and equally proficient trainmen who could drive through in record time. *Speed, speed and more SPEED!* It was trains

The mammoth railroad bridge spanning the Ohio River between Cairo, Ill., and East Cairo, Ky.

like these that Casey longed to haul—so that he could show even Lee Chandler there were records to be broken and new records to be set.

There had been times when so much wheat rolled into New Orleans that it sprouted in the cars before it could be loaded upon ocean-going vessels. But enormous and complete dock facilities, such as the Stuyvesant docks with their accompanying elevators, were gradually making it possible to handle as much grain as the trains could haul into the southern seaport.

Such accomplishments fired the imagination of Casey Jones and increased the intensity of his desire to ally himself with this great railroad whose amazing growth was due in such large measure to the genius and driving force of its management.

Until 1888 the weakest link in an otherwise perfectly coordinated chain was the ferryboat crossing between Cairo, Illinois, and East Cairo, Kentucky. When the monster railroad bridge was flung six miles across the Ohio, high enough for the largest battleship to pass beneath it, this last deficiency was overcome.

And then, through the acquisition of the Gulf and Ship Island Railway and other feeder lines in the deep south, the Illinois Central solved an important economic operating problem by bringing back the grain cars with north bound loads of other commodities. . . .

At last came the layover at Jackson, with a good long rest—and Jane Brady. No lover was ever so bashful as he. But he had become desperate, and he fanned his courage to the point where he could bare his heart and mind to this girl who had so completely and hopelessly captivated him.

When he caught and held her two hands in both of his and saw that she was not disposed to draw away, he suddenly blurted, looking at her hungrily:

"Janie—darling—can we live on half my salary?"

With becoming restraint she looked up slowly and gazed intently into his eyes.

"Do you think it fair," she said quizzically, "to expect that?"

"God knows it isn't. But I love you, Janie. I can't do without you."

No mistaking the love that vibrated in his voice, that shone in his eyes. He trembled with the very force of it. And in what lay behind his question, a thing to which he clung in this crisis that meant happiness or misery to him, she read one thing—Loyalty. No, she could not expect him, under any circumstances, to neglect his parents.

"I suppose we can, if we try," she said simply, and found herself happily enfolded in his arms, her lips pressed warmly against his.

And so it was settled, and on the morning of November 25, 1886, Casey Jones and Jane Brady were married in St. Mary's church at Jackson, Tennessee.

CHAPTER XXIV

THE HONEYMOON

CASEY accepted almost as a matter of course an order from F. L. Holland, his master mechanic, delivered by call-boy to Mrs. Brady's boarding house, to report at Artesia, Mississippi. This occurred within an hour after the wedding. Casey hurried to the master mechanic's office.

"Artesia?" he inquired, protestingly. "Why Artesia? That's 'way out among the mosquitoes and bullfrogs. I got a wife to think of now, you know."

Holland grinned.

"If you don't want to take your bride down there, you can leave your name on the call-board and see her whenever chance wants to do you a good turn. Which won't be often this time of year."

"I'll take Artesia," said Casey glumly. "What is it?"

Then came the glad surprise.

"A month or so on a work-train-extra working out of Artesia. Report to Sam Merritt tomorrow, find you and your wife some comfortable quarters and live in heaven for a month or two. After that it may be hell and you'll look back to this moment and thank me."

A month firing on a work-train-extra! A railroad man could not have been given a better wedding present!

At home every night with his wife, without having to
hold himself in readiness for long runs and long periods
of absence.

Next night Casey and Jane found themselves in a
spacious, old-fashioned room, with an enormous four-
poster bed sheltered by a tester; a fireplace, and walls
graced by dim portraits of some of their host's fore-
bears. The room was in a typical old Southern planta-
tion house, set among hoary liveoaks and waxy magnolia
trees, their host being one Mortimer Ellis, enterprising
planter, breeder of beef cattle, and patron of the M. &
O. Railroad.

Yet, even in this blissful, undisturbed environment,
the thoughts of Casey Jones constantly reverted to the
Illinois Central! It would not be correct to say that
his thoughts strayed from Jane, for she was his inspira-
tion, and his very life centered about her. But he
could not banish from his mind his overwhelming
ambition as a railroad man; and he was forever seeing
the image of Lee Chandler running away from old Bill
Flickenger and even beating Bose Lashley. Bose at
least had tried, had got out of his hog as much as the
old kettle could give. . . .

It was a moonless, star-studded night in late November. No vagrant breath stirred the lush, dew-
saturated foliage, seen only as black shadow masses that
possessed peculiarly fathomless liquid depths. Such a
hush brooded over the world as one in the deep South

learns to love and wait for and revel in. A cricket or two chirped lazily against a strident but muted background chorus of a myriad other singing insects, and far away a lone whippoorwill, yielding to an autumnal urge to revive springtime's unforgotten joys, called insistently, without pause.

"Hear that whippoorwill?" Casey broke the silence. "When I get me a hog on the I. C. I'm going to make her quill sound just like that when I come rolling into wherever we're living. You'll know it's your old man hurrying home to his Sugarfoots."

The speech startled Jane.

"When you are on the I. C.?" she repeated. "What do you mean?"

This may have been a queer time for Casey to launch upon what had become his fondest dream, but once started he waxed eloquent.

Poor Janie, however, could not be expected to appreciate the perplexing situation at New Orleans brought on by the inability of the ship lines to clear the elevators; nor could she be expected to evince any great interest in the fact that the capacity of the Levee and Poydras yards could no longer be depended upon.

Jane was a practical minded young woman, intensely interested in the success and advancement of her husband. She knew that company officials held him in high esteem and that with his ability and personality there was no limit to what he might accomplish. But go over to another railroad just when he was about to be moved to the righthand side of a locomotive cab?—That did not make sense.

Her husband tried his best to kindle in her some of the fire of his own enthusiasm over what the captains of the other railroad were accomplishing.

"And then, Janie, think of it!" the bridegroom cried. "Their cars don't go back north empty. They've built up a traffic there that is the wonder of the railroad world."

She watched him steadily, her pretty face betraying no emotion. He asked suddenly:

"Aren't you interested?"

"Go on," she returned noncommittally. "I'm listening."

"Bananas," he said as if the one word were sufficient to explain everything. "The I. C. has built up an import business from Honduras and other South American countries in bananas that just about supplies the American market. Bananas come into New Orleans by the shipload. The cars that carry wheat and corn south come back filled with bananas. Why, the I. C. has even installed warehouses along its trunkline to care for the millions of stems of fruit in freezing weather."

Her regard by this time had become one of open incredulity. Towering elevators—bananas—what reasons were these for quitting one employment to take up another?

"Casey Jones," she said sharply, "if I thought you

were serious I'd catch the first rattler back to Jackson and mamma."

Jane had been brought up in a railroad boarding house and had absorbed much of its atmosphere; "rattler" came as naturally from her lips as the word train.

"Sugarfoots!" he protested. "You wouldn't leave me!"

"Well," she temporized, "maybe not. But I'd at least take you back and have your head examined. Think of losing your seniority. Of having to start over again and fire four more years."

He had thought of it—long and earnestly—but realized that this was no time to argue the matter with his Sugarfoots.

"Going to fetch me a hot dinner today at the south crossing?"

"Have I ever failed?"

"You never will, sweetheart. But we may be a bit late today. The bridge across Pipe Creek, south of town, calls for a lot of work yet—new piling and so on. We got to make it safe for heavy trains. Old Sam lets me handle the throttle most of the time; I'll give you the whippoorwill call in time so you can get to the crossing."

Jane did not hear the whippoorwill note from the work train's whistle that day for the simple reason that Casey had to conserve every ounce of steam to bring in his engine, minus tender and cars. Hours after time for the work train to show up, Janie, with fear clutching at her heart, was waiting at the south crossing with a dinner that had long since grown cold. She could not believe her eyes when she saw the tenderless locomotive come limping past, her husband alone in the cab and grinning cheerfully down at her.

Speechlessly, she held up his dinner basket, and he reached down and took it from her hand. He had time to yell:

"What you think of my first engine run? Most of the work train cars are in the bed of Pipe Creek, honey. I managed to hold the old mudhen on the edge and ease her over until the tender uncoupled. Nobody hurt much! S'long!"

The tenderless locomotive retained barely enough steam to make Artesia, where Casey filed a full report of the collapse of the bridge——, luckily, not under the weight of one of the fast passenger trains.

That night he told Jane: "Sugarfoots, that settles it. I'm on my way to Jackson and the I. C."

She began a weak protest.

"Your—your seniority—" and fell silent.

"Seniority be hanged!" he retorted grandly. "I already got my place on the I. C., and I bet I'll be running an engine in less than two years."

CHAPTER XXV

THE I. C. CLAIMS CASEY

CASEY was correct in his prophecy as to when he would begin drawing an engineman's pay on the Illinois Central. The records of that railroad show that he entered its employ on March first, 1888, and drew his first engineman's pay February first, 1890, as engineer on a switch engine in Chester Street yard, Jackson, Tennessee.

In the very beginning of his connection with the Illinois Central the young railroader was put through strict examinations and rigid tests, and his talent was quickly recognized. During the course of his first preliminary examinations Casey voluntarily stressed the economic importance of speed in moving trains. Faster schedules meant better business and that's what the I. C. wanted. The master mechanic, who tried to be stern and strictly official, thought it an extremely unusual examination; and the impression was not in the least dispelled when the unabashed Casey smiled whimsically and said:

"And there's one hoghead on this railroad I mean to show how to run an engine one of these days."

"Who's that?" the M. M. demanded.

Casey drawled: "A guy by the name of Lee Chandler."

The master mechanic stared.

"My boy, when you get to driving a locomotive like Lee Chandler—if you ever do get to driving a locomotive on this man's railroad—" He stopped suddenly, suspecting from Casey's expression and mien that there was some background of rivalry here of which he was ignorant. He ended by asking: "You know Lee Chandler?"

"Sure I know Lee. We're good friends. I just got it fixed in my mind that one of these days I'm goin' to beat the best runnin' record he ever made."

The master mechanic grinned.

"If you can do that and stick to the rails," he said, *"we will make you a present of the right of way from Chicago to New Orleans."*

Before many years had passed the M. M. was reminded of that promise and, for the first memorable trip of the famous locomotive, No. 638, saw to it that it was made good; that Casey Jones had practically undisputed control over the road between Chicago and Water Valley, Mississippi, which was close enough to keep to the spirit of the promise.

Despite Jane's fears the change turned out to be so satisfactory from a financial standpoint that she could not come back at her jubilant husband with the time honored feminine retort, "I told you so." Furthermore, she soon saw that the young giant commanded the respect of his superiors for reasons that had nothing to do with Boomer Bill Driscoll or like exploits.

Certificate No. 145

Illinois Central Railroad Company.

Jackson 3/12 189.5

CERTIFICATE OF EXAMINATION ON AIR BRAKE PRACTICE.

THIS IS TO CERTIFY That J. A. Jones, *Locomotive Engineer,*

on Jackson *District has this day passed satisfactory examination on AIR BRAKE*

PRACTICE, and that he is fully qualified to handle and operate AIR BRAKE EQUIPMENT, in use

on this road at the present time

WM. RENSHAW, Supt. of Machinery.

Examination conducted by R. W. Davis, *Traveling Engineer,*

For example, when the airbrake was beginning to be accepted by the major railroad systems as a genuine improvement, Casey Jones stood an examination relative to the mechanism and passed with flying colors. And he did not hesitate to point out to the examiner:

"When the airbrake is perfected it'll be the biggest thing ever invented to help along the quick movement of trains."

"What's the matter with it now?" the examiner wanted to know with some show of hostility. He had worked hard to get the company to adopt and install the new device, and he was not disposed to admit any defects in it.

"You really want me to go into that?" returned Casey.

"Go ahead."

"Straight air," Casey began, "is not the thing. The compressors don't provide enough pressure. Not enough freight cars are equipped with it to do much good. Then in an emergency the whole thing is liable to fail."—And so on, going into technical details which absorbed the gathering of brass hats but could be of no possible interest to the general reader. It may be said, briefly, that the shortcomings pointed out by Casey during his examination are what later were overcome in the present triple-valve Westinghouse brake.

For a moment Casey fell silent. A memory flashed into his mind. He heard himself asking in changing voice: "Why does steam squirt from them spigots when you all slow down?" How shyly he had asked the question!

· "Spigots!" he uttered unconsciously.

"What's that?" demanded the examiner.

Casey came to himself with a start.

"Why, sir, if it's not improper to offer the suggestion—if we can get the proper kind of brake and in addition have some system of superheatin' our steam——"

He was interrupted. A member of the company spoke up emphatically.

"Young man, you have an idea there. And you are not alone. The superheater and perhaps some sort of booster are going to be the biggest boons the railroad has known since the discovery of steam—along with a perfected airbrake."

Casey was voted the award without further questioning.

CHAPTER XXVI

ENGINEER CASEY JONES

WELL, I'll be doggoned!" burst from a transfixed young giant known as Casey Jones.

Lashley's unemotional countenance broke into a quiet grin.

"You will be," said he, "if you don't keep my kite flying."

Casey let out a sudden yell that would have been a credit to the stentorian voice of Runt Chandler.

"Whoopee! The old hellbender engine driver from the fork of the creek couldn't stay away from his old fireboy! Are you sure enough an engineman on this road?"

"Does it look like I'm on my way to pick strawberries? Maybe I came down to help keep you straight, you big apple knocker."

Casey deliberately overwhelmed his friend by throwing his long arms around his slender figure and executing a sort of Indian war dance. Bose struggled free and dodged back to a safe distance.

Casey grinned at him happily.

"We're driving north together, are we?" he said.

Lashley regarded him sourly.

"Heaven help me," he replied, "it looks like I can't help myself."

"Then I tell you what," said Casey. "Let's give Lee Chandler hell."

Perhaps they didn't give Lee Chandler hell on that run, but with the locomotive in top condition, the trip was highly satisfactory.

At Ft. Jefferson the view was reversed for them— they looked across at the M. & O. right of way instead of contemplating, from the M. & O. track, Lee Chandler running away from them and thumbing his nose derisively.

During the comparatively brief time Casey Jones spent firing on the Illinois Central, he became thoroughly familiar with a great railroad system that suited him perfectly. We know that he was already fully qualified to drive an engine when he went over to the I. C. By the time he had served his novitiate and was given his engineman's ticket he was as capable an engineer as any veteran of the road—a road that was noted for its famous engineers such as the Chandlers, the Gaffneys, Neudorfer, Hunt, Nourse, Watkins, Bosma, Weldon, Baxter, Staley, Harrington and Wooley, whose names are emblazoned on the tablets of memory among old-time railroaders everywhere.

The engine that Casey Jones drove on his first run as engineer in February 1892 will be designated by the number 736. Its real identifying number is not of record. It is known, however, that she was one of the saturated steam mudhens and was reputed to be a jonah.

To take such a locomotive and equal or exceed the accomplishments of other engineers with their favorite hogs was something to be proud of. Casey Jones took No. 736 as she was, and he was never known to complain or admit any defects in her during all the time that she was assigned to him.

It is dazzling to think of the speeds that were attained by those old engineers in view of the light rails, the lightly ballasted roadbeds, the types of locomotives and other factors at that time as compared with the tremendously superior conditions existing today. Even with all such details brought to modern perfection few railroads permit their fastest trains to attain a speed in excess of seventy miles per hour.

Back in the good old days the hoghead pulled the throttle to his chest and hoped the old kettle wouldn't climb the rails. Speeds of 100 to 112 miles per hour were accomplished on many a memorable run.

The crack express trains were given the rating of first class. If for no other reason the mail contracts alone would have made this necessary. But fast freights with their valuable cargoes were the real backbone of the railroad, and any engineer was proud to have such a run.

It was Engine 736 that Casey was running on three outstanding occasions remembered by many an old rail.

The first of these notable events was when Casey kept his promise to "show Lee Chandler how to run an engine." And the occasion was Casey Jones' very first run as a regular engineer!

It was one of the times when No. 52, northbound freight, was running as a "pawpaw special"; that is, she was loaded with bananas. She was strung out along the main line in a half-dozen sections. These sections pulled out of Chester Street yard, at Jackson, Tennessee, approximately ten minutes apart. Casey, with 736, was coupled to the first section; Lee Chandler's mogul was dragging the second, and Bose Lashley was with section 3.

When Lee Chandler arrived at Mounds, Illinois, the northern terminal of their run, after making pretty nearly a record run himself, he received what he admitted was a distinct and convincing jolt.

He stared incredulously at the train register on seeing that first 52, Casey's train, had checked in twenty minutes ahead of the arrival of second 52, his own train.

But capping this surprise was an insolent note, signed by Casey, pinned to the train register. It read:

"Fella, you ought to been with me and learned how to run an engine."

CHAPTER XXVII

FLIGHT OF THE IRISH MAIL

THE rough and ready ballad *Flight of the Irish Mail*, commemorates the second of these events. There was a run that sent Casey Jones and 736 through Jackson and on south to Water Valley before he turned back home again. On his regular run he doubled out of Mounds, Illinois, which made Jackson—and home—his layover terminal. But on this particular occasion there was no layover at Jackson. Out of Jackson they rolled within a few minutes after arrival for the long run to the Mississippi terminal. The rail of those days was accustomed to long hours of driving labor.

When Casey and 736 started north again they had to drag the despised local mixed train, known in the vernacular as the "Irish Mail," from Water Valley to Jackson. This run became historic.

When the local left Water Valley it was scheduled for no less than seven stops to unload and load freight, and was subject to flag stop at any station where a passenger might want to get aboard and ride perhaps no farther than the next station. The Irish Mail enjoyed few rights, and her operating schedule was uncertain.

One rule she had to adhere to, and that was to keep out of the way of all other trains.

Casey pulled out of Water Valley yard in excess of regulation speed, and the fireboy had his first hunch that they were starting on a trip that would call for "all the kiyi the old kettle would stand"; which meant almost unremittent swinging of the coal scoop.

And all for the meek and lowly Irish Mail, least considered of trains!

But here is where the drama began. In another twenty minutes No. 24, fast northbound express and mail train, would be pulling out behind the mixed local. Dick Clark was No. 24's hoghead; not the Dick Clark known in later years, but a predecessor famous as a runner in the early 90's. Normally, No. 24 might have been expected to overtake No. 82, the Irish Mail's official designation, and find it sitting on a sidetrack not farther north than Waterford, and to have gone by to run ahead of the local at that point.

However, when No. 24's conductor and engineer registered and got their clearance at the Water Valley dispatcher's office, they were told something they never had been told before.

"Look out for No. 82 north of Abbeville!"

In justified astonishment, Dick Clark demanded to be told why. The last thing he had to look out for was the Irish Mail.

The dispatcher explained: "The way they're running, you're liable to find 'em piled up somewhere on the right of way."

To summarize this remarkable running feat, the Irish Mail left the southern terminal twenty minutes ahead of a speedy mail and express train, and by gaining on the express's fast running time was enabled to make all its local stops, taking the siding for three southbound trains, and finally arrive in the yard of the northern terminal with ten minutes to spare ahead of the mail train.

This performance excited widespread comment up and down the entire trunkline of the Illinois Central and throughout the Midwest and Mississippi Valley. Once again Casey found himself thrust into a position of prominence that had a much more vital significance than the notoriety that followed his conquest of Boomer Bill Driscoll.

As often as Casey had been in the roundhouse at Water Valley, Mississippi, he had failed to notice a figure whose eyes never left him. Intent upon his own business, Casey never saw the little black man in extremely dirty blue overalls who peered at him from ashpit or between the drivers of an engine on which he was working; always in obscurity, always silent, an insect that might have been trodden upon by a careless foot. This humble individual never presumed to approach and address the famous Casey Jones.

Casey was all the more puzzled, therefore, when

shortly after the feat of the Irish Mail he began to hear a doggerel ballad with a curiously familiar quality which he was told had emanated from the Water Valley roundhouse. Casey had never seen Wallace Saunders at Water Valley and felt sure that had the little negro been there he would have seen him. The song tickled Casey, nevertheless, and he learned most of it by heart.

Up to this time he had never come face to face with Lee Chandler since he had run so far ahead of him into Mounds on first 52. Then they came together one day in the roundhouse at Jackson. A half-dozen or so other rails were present.

Casey came upon his brother engineer unawares. Catching Chandler by a shoulder he swung him around and holding him thus stuck thumb to nose and deliberately wiggled his fingers in Chandler's face.

"This ain't Ft. Jefferson, Bud," he said, "but you know what I mean."

Startled for a moment, Chandler quickly recovered his wits and laughed heartily. He turned to the group and declared:

"Fellas, look at this guy. He's the fella that let his hog run away with him and couldn't stop her till she steamed out. Better keep a lookout for him behind or sometime he'll bump you off the right of way."

Casey in turn grinned companionably.

"Bud, I made all my stops and did my running in between, like any good hoghead would. But I can pick up that little old 736 hog any time and still give you

pointers about engine running.   Ever hear a song that
goes like this?"   And in a hoarse, rather unmusical but
pleasing voice, Casey roared forth:

> "Out of Water Valley yard rolled 82;
>   Says Casey Jones: I'll drive her through.
>   No. 24's stepping right on our tail,
>   And we got to keep ahead of the Limited Mail.

> "Casey says: 'Fireboy, the steam's too low;
>   This may be the local but she shan't run slow.'
>   Fireboy says: 'Casey, she won't stand no more;
>   The Irish Mail never has beat 24.' "

It became evident at once that, despite its freshness,
every one of the rails present not only knew the circumstance that inspired the song but also was familiar with
all or some of the stanzas.   First one and then another
took up the burden and soon the entire gathering were
shouting a lusty chorus with Casey Jones the leader.

> "No. 24 was hauling the Government mail,
>   And Dick Clark knew he must not fail.
>   Somewheres he'd pass that local freight,
>   And the Government mail would not be late.

> "Out of Water Valley yard the Fast Mail raced,
>   Through Cathey's Cut 82 she chased;
>   Through Cathey's Cut the Fast Mail sped,
>   But the Irish Mail was far ahead."

Here Lee Chandler broke in with an interruption, yelling at the top of his lungs to make himself heard.

"His hog was running away with him again, fellas. Good thing No. 24 wasn't ahead of him."

Immediately he took up again the burden of the song.

"The line was cleared for the Fast Express——"

And here Casey stopped the singing—if singing the tumult could be called.

"That's a durn lie. Everything had to take the hole for 24 anyhow—except me. I kept out of her way." Lifting his voice again, he resumed:

"The line was cleared for the Fast Express,
    And her hogger was doing his daggone best.
He says to his fireboy: 'What shall we do?
For nowheres ahead can I see 82.'

"He says to the fireboy: '82's so slow
    We ought to run around her a hour ago.'
Fireboy says: 'Mister, 82 can't fly,
So we'll be a whizzing past her by and by.' "

At this point most of the bunch had run out of recollection of the stanzas, but Casey wouldn't stop.

"You guys quittin' on me, hey? Well, you got to listen to this last verse. It's a lulu."

"Seven stops were made by 82,
  While 24 balled the jack right through——
  Chasing 82 and burning up the rails,
  But she couldn't catch up with the Irish Mail."

The noisy seance ended with Lee Chandler throwing an arm around Casey's shoulders and exclaiming:

"Fella, come on to my boarding-house and let's have dinner together."

But Casey shook his head.

"You know I got a wife that's lookin' for me. Her cooking's not boarding-house cooking, so you come with me."

"I'll do that, taking a chance on Mrs. Jones throwing me out."

CHAPTER XXVIII

THE WRECK AT TOONE

THE third and final episode in the career of Casey Jones' 736 was the wreck at Toone, resulting in a queer lawsuit and the retirement of the jonah locomotive as a road engine.

Approximately twenty-two miles south of Jackson, in Tennessee, was a station noted on the time table as Toone, then composed almost solely of a long passing track and landscape.

Casey, with 736 dragging train 52, regular northbound freight, rolled northward, his mind carrying no weightier problem than the thought that he was on his way home to Janie. He was so far ahead of his running time that he had the old mudhen throttled down to thirty miles per hour.

Approaching Toone, as he reached for the whistle cord to sound the long station signal, he espied, first, a faint hovering fog of coal smoke, and next, a northbound train resting on the passing track, far ahead.

He rightly concluded that the train was the Irish Mail—which should have arrived at Jackson long ago—but he was mistaken in believing that the local was waiting for his train to pass.

Casey was inclined to impart a derisive note to his

whistle's blast, to jeer the crew of the Irish Mail for being no nearer home than Toone. It would remind them how he had driven this same Irish Mail through to the terminal only a short time previously.

But in a flash—impending disaster! Instead of seizing the whistle cord, one hand dropped to the airbrake handle, and the other jammed in the throttle. The caboose of the supposedly waiting train was backing out upon the main line, directly in his path!

Casey's heart did a somersault. He yelled at his fireman: "Unload!" But the fireboy was too frightened to stir.

Then Casey steadied. Eight air equipped cars directly behind 736 gave assurance of considerable braking power. If not to stop before the bump, at least to avert a bad crash.

Next instant 736's quill was shrieking frantically for brakes.

Her air, which up to now during the run had responded to every service application, failed utterly in this emergency. The reservoirs were as empty as if the compressor had never moved a stroke.

Running true to form, 736 was not to be shaken from her hoodoo.

All that Casey could do now was throw the engine into reverse, open wide the sand dome, and try to feed steam to her in the exact degree that would check the train's speed as quickly as possible without locking the driving wheels. Once more he looked across at his terrified fireman and yelled, "Unload, you damn' fool!"

Then 736 plowed into the caboose.

The most serious consequences of the wreck were, fortunately, a splintered doghouse, a blocked main line, and a lawsuit that cost the company $1200. The lawsuit was a curious one. It was brought by a clergyman, a passenger on the local train. His Bible was lost and never recovered, and that was the sole basis of his claim for damages.

When 736 came out of the shops her cowcatcher and pilot wheels had been removed. She was thus transformed into a total adhesion type switch engine, banished to some yard, and lost sight of as a road engine.

Casey's recollection alone provides the information as to what immediately followed the wreck at Toone. He had several days layoff, during which time some detail took him to Water Valley, Mississippi,—to the roundhouse.

"What caused me to go to Water Valley," Casey told the writer, "I can't remember. But, resting on the turntable in front of the roundhouse I saw something."

It was the biggest locomotive he had ever seen. It was shiny new from the hands of its maker, dwarfing squat 736 to a level of crawling insignificance. The style and sheer massiveness of this terrific power machine profoundly impressed the young engineer.

"It was the type of engine I'd been looking forward to ever since I'd known the railroad. I recognized it as soon as I saw it. A hog specially designed for speed and long heavy drags."

Casey Jones' name has been rightly associated with the famous No. 638. Here was her physical counterpart.

The engine was a Rogers consolidation, 2-8-0 class: which is to say that it was equipped with two pilot wheels, eight drivers and no trailers. The Illinois Central had acquired thirty-eight of them, numbered serially 601–638. The number of the engine at Water Valley that attracted Casey was 622. Nos. 601–621 were to be operated on the North End, Jackson, Tennessee to Mounds, Illinois, and Nos. 622–638 on the South End, Jackson, Tennessee to Water Valley, Mississippi. These locomotives were for heavy freight duty.*

As Casey stared fascinated at the monster 622, into the depths of his absorption a peculiar sensation penetrated. It became a conviction that somebody was watching him. He glanced around.

"Well, dog my cats if it ain't Wallace. You black scoundrel, what you doing here?"

Wallace's overalls were indescribably ragged and dirty and reeking with black grease.

The monkeylike countenance was working spasmodically, unmistakably expressing a pleasure that no words could convey.

"Us is engine wiper, please suh, Mist' Casey."

* See Appendix, note 15.

"Still a deacon in good standing?"

The black boy's face clouded. He glanced away.

"Aha!" cried Casey. "Backslider, hey? What is it—women—dice?"

Wallace squirmed. This catechism plainly was painful to him. But the eyes of his idol were boring into him and he could not evade.

"None o' them things, Mist' Casey!" he finally muttered.

"Not women or—or the rollin' ivories?" repeated Casey with mock severity.

Wallace was miserable.

"No, suh."

"Then what started you on the downward path?"

The boy swallowed hard, his little round eyes glancing at Casey, then darting away. Then he said:

"Gin."

Casey studied the wretched looking little darky.

"Wallace," he presently asked, "you making up any more songs?"

This change of subject caused Wallace to become articulate.

"No, suh. But us had some funny dreams—dreams 'bout you, Mist' Casey."

"If it had been about anything else," said Casey, "I'd say it was the gin. Tell us."

Wallace became impressively solemn.

"You was lyin' still, Mist' Casey," he said, "an' a bale o' hay was on top o' you."

"Well, now!" exclaimed Casey. "That's something. You got me under a bale of hay. Anything more?"

"No, suh. Exceptin' there was a lot o' shelled corn scattered 'round."

Again Casey grew severe.

"Boy," he soberly charged, "you leave that nigger gin alone."

CHAPTER XXIX

CHICAGO 1893—COLUMBIAN EXPOSITION

THE enormous new Rogers consolidated Casey had seen at Water Valley had remained constantly in his thoughts, and he was overjoyed when he was assigned to one of that type, a counterpart of famous 638. He was given Engine No. 618 and sent to the north end, the change enabling Jane and the children to move from Water Valley and reestablish themselves at Jackson.

Casey Jones had been an engineer two years. The brass hats had never openly patted him on the back in recognition of the things he had done and the record he was making, but he was soon to have a signal token of what they thought of him.

Less than two years an engineer and he was assigned to a fast freight run between Champaign, Illinois, and Chicago—a run so crowded and busy that only the best engineers were assigned to it.

During the World's Columbian Exposition in 1893, he operated a shuttle train carrying passengers between Van Buren Street and the Fair Grounds. But this did not accord with his conception of railroading, and at his request he was sent back to the Champaign-Chicago run. During this period he had many opportunities to visit the Fair; and in the Transportation Building among the exhibits of the Illinois Central Railroad Company, he saw for the first time Engine No. 638.

No. 638 was all aglow with oil and lacquer, and shone resplendently. Perfect—to all outward appearances. Yet, as Casey said, "The instant I clapped eyes on her I knew she would perform as well as she looked. I made up my mind then and there she was going to be mine. Janie was with me at the time, visiting the Fair."

"Why," Casey once was asked, "if your 618 was a counterpart of 638, why didn't she satisfy you?"

"Because," replied Casey, "in a flock of engines, like the company put into service at that time, there's bound to be one or two that simply won't work right. And besides no two are just alike. Old 618 was a good hog in her way, but I've always had a suspicion she was turned over to me to see if I could iron the seams out of her. Nobody else wanted her."

Casey Jones had indeed made up his mind that he was going to have locomotive 638 for his very own. He got a layoff and deadheaded down to Jackson to the master mechanic who had promised him the right of way if he ever beat Lee Chandler's running record. Outside the M. M.'s door he stopped long enough to wipe an exultant grin from his face and murmur to himself: "I'm going to make this jaybird sweat."

He did not pause to knock but entered as if he belonged. It was a busy office and the M. M. looked up to regard him sourly. At once he recognized the new-comer, and his scowl vanished. Then his look became speculative. One could almost hear him thinking, "This fella's got something up his sleeve. I got to be careful."

Casey saw a vacant chair and sat down without being invited.

"Well," drawled he, "you promised me the right of way once, Chicago to New Orleans, on one condition. Have I earned it?"

"Casey Jones," returned the master mechanic, "You've come in here to bring me more trouble. What th' hell you want?"

Casey's cheerfulness was not in the least abashed. He grinned in friendly fashion as much as to say, "Cheer up, boss, this ain't going to sink you but it's sure going to make you swim and tread water."

"You been to the Chicago Fair?" began Casey.

"Two-three times," admitted the M. M.

"Of course you've seen the company's exhibit there. There's a little old engine in it—lemme see—I think it's number is 638. Nobody would ever want that hog, would they?" he innocently concluded.

The M. M. stared at him. He said bluntly: "You do, don't you? That's why you've come here. Well, if you get it, what?"

Casey's grin widened.

"Why," he said, "I aim to make a splash. I want everybody from here to Kingdom Come to know I got the best hog rolling on rails."

The M. M. assured him that there would probably be no difficulty in having 638 assigned to him.

"Fine," Casey beamed. "So how about letting me borrow the right of way a couple of days?"

With thunderstruck expression the M. M. again stared.

"Don't forget," Casey said. "I got your promise. The way those six hundred hogs have been assigned, 638 will go to the South End. Me—myself—*I* want to run her from the spur in the Transportation Building at the Fair all the way to Water Valley."

The M. M. gestured helplessly. He groaned:

"Was there ever such a nut! I see you mean it. You know that's five divisions. I'll have to take it up with the general superintendent at Chicago."

"And if he hesitates," Casey reminded, "mention my first run with a pawpaw special when I beat Lee Chandler and ran into Mounds twenty minutes ahead of the advertised."

"Seven stops were made by 82,
  While 24 balled the jack right through——
  Chasing 82 and burning up the rails,
  But she couldn't catch up with the Irish Mail."

And out of that early, unthinking promise to grant an engineer the right of way over a long trunkline, grew one of the most remarkable occurrences in the history of the railroad; a signal recognition of Casey Jones' outstanding genius as engineer and railroad man.

CHAPTER XXX

A PROMISE KEPT

CASEY JONES' extraordinary request was presented at the general offices in Chicago, and after
the first moment of speechless astonishment it excited
considerable merriment among the officials. There was
much facetious speculation as to why this irrepressible
but reliable young engineer should make such an unusual request, some expressing the opinion that it was
intended as a practical joke. Others, however, pointing
to Casey's record and reputation, insisted that he was
probably in dead earnest. All agreed that such a request
was ridiculous and ordinarily should be denied.

Then one high official, with a flash of intuition,
brought the matter quickly to a head.

"All joking aside, gentlemen," said William Renshaw, "this man Jones has proved he knows his business
and can be trusted. Let's take him at his word, without
question, and give him the engine with orders to drive it
through to Water Valley. If he wants to show off, all
right. Afterward we will have him make some tests
with extra heavy drags."

During this interim the importance of the ultimate
adoption of the newly conceived "Tonnage System" was

199

indicated by an experience Casey had while driving south with No. 618.

There was a certain conductor, the one who wore a long, black coat, derby, celluloid collar and black string tie to match—an incongruous personage whom we shall call Slim. Some of Slim's fellow workers said he was a kleptomaniac. Casey Jones declared him bluntly to be a damn' thief. On one run he carried away an entire crated buggy, which was never accounted for; and another time he filled the possumbelly of the doghouse with a crate of geese that never reached their consignee.

These things, although known to Casey, did not come directly under his observation, as he did not handle the waybills; but on this occasion when Slim tossed a small bag of dried beans into a freight car and closed and sealed the door, Casey wondered.

"That car's an empty," said Casey.

"Like hell," retorted Slim. "Didn't you just see me load it?"

"Load it!" exclaimed Casey. "With a bag of beans you picked up with one hand?"

Slim shook a long and knuckly finger under Casey's nose.

"Listen, fella," he said. "The lighter your drag the quicker you get into the terminal, what? I'm the brains, ain't I? These waybills show we have eighteen loaded high cars, and I guarantee they won't stall your old teakettle. If you don't go to sleep we'll drag in on the advertised."

Some time later Casey, alone with his trainmaster, gave voice to the perplexity that the foregoing circumstance had aroused in his mind.

"How come," he asked, "you can toss a bag of beans into an empty high car, seal the door and rate it a load?"

"Who did that?" the trainmaster demanded.

Casey smiled. "I ain't saying anybody did. I'm offering a hypothetical case. I reckon it costs this railroad a hell of a lot of money to drag cars around that are supposed to be loaded and ain't got nothin' in 'em."

The trainmaster picked up two or three letters held together by a wire clip. Glancing at them, he favored Casey with a cryptic smile.

"Casey," he said, "the railroads have got to straighten that out pretty soon. How would you like to have the job?"

Casey considered. "Maybe," he said finally.

"Well," said the trainmaster, "you're going to get that 638 locomotive at the World's Fair. I got an order here that's going to let you run her from Chicago to Water Valley, over five divisions. By the time you get to Water Valley you'll think the I. C. belongs to you, hey?"

Casey had stood up and was pacing up and down the room. His face was ashine with delighted satisfaction.

"You ain't joshing me?" he shouted. "You mean I got that 638 hog and can run it to Water Valley? Mister, what do you want that I can drag out by the roots and hand you?"

"Ha," returned the trainmaster with a tone and manner that cooled Casey's enthusiasm, exciting his suspicion. "You don't know what you've let yourself in for."

Casey gazed at the file of letters in the trainmaster's hand. He dropped back into his chair.

"You tell me, Mister."

The trainmaster's manner was exasperating. He pulled open a drawer of his desk and dropped the file of letters into it.

"Wait till you get to Water Valley with your 638 hog. You'll learn all about it."

The show engine in the Illinois Central exhibit at the World's Fair was assigned to Casey Jones. Accompanying the notification was an order that permitted him to run the locomotive from the Transportation Building in the Fair Grounds to Water Valley, keeping clear only of first class trains.

Casey laid them under Jane's nose.

"Look," he said.

She looked. She read them through; read them the second time, then commenced to cry.

"Durn it!" exclaimed Casey. "I hoped you'd help me laugh. Please tell me, honey, why this good news should make you weep."

She looked up, smiling through the tears.

"It's because I'm so happy. I objected to you coming over to the I. C., and Casey, my darling, I was wrong."

Casey took Janie into his arms. He smoothed her

hair and lifted her up to where he could kiss her without having to stoop.

"Listen, sweetheart," he whispered, "when you're ready to admit some other things you're wrong about, why, I——"

She checked him by wriggling like an eel from his embrace, standing confronting him with clenched fists and flashing eyes.

"Casey Jones, I'm not wrong about anything!"

Casey gazed at her a moment, then took the easiest way out.

"Sugarfoots," he said, "you're always right."

For some reason that made her mad.

"I'm not!" she cried, and stormed out of the room.

Casey rubbed his chin reflectively and ruminated.

"Durn funny, but I've never run a engine that wasn't just like that."

CHAPTER XXXI

RUN OF THE 638

THE men who took Engine No. 638 out of the Transportation Building to Burnside Shops deferred to the tall young fellow who eagerly watched every step of the operation. Casey, boy-like, could not resist the temptation to collect some of the flags, streamers and other decorative gewgaws with which the Fair grounds abounded, and drape them appropriately here and there on his new locomotive; and at Burnside, where the engine was checked, fired and made ready for her long run, he would not permit any of her showy embellishments to be removed.

Engine 638 was on her way south. Casey Jones looked across his cab and grinned at his excited fireboy.

"What you think of her, Bud?" he asked.

"Looks great, Mr. Casey," replied the youngster, "but wait 'til I see how much coal I got to scoop."

But he did not have to bail many black diamonds. The locomotive was, in trainmen's parlance, "running light." That is to say, locomotive and tender were not encumbered by so much as one car.

An engine "running light" can shake herself from the rails if driven at too high a speed; the drag of a car or two is needed for ballast. But 638 proceeded along at a lively enough rate to click off on the rail joints a tune that one heard everywhere in Chicago known as the *Hoochie-Koochie*. A woman dancer, Little Egypt, pirouetted to it before admiring hundreds at the Fair.

And there was another tune that got under 638's wheels and sang to the engine crew. It was a brand new song that everybody was singing—*After the Ball*.

Over five divisions Casey Jones drove 638 on its way to Water Valley, and at every terminal he had a new fireman.

"Bud," he shouted to each in turn, "Ain't she sweet? Wouldn't she hump herself with a good drag strung out behind her? All she wants is plenty of kiyi."

It was not until 638 arrived at the end of the first division out of Chicago that Casey realized what a sensation the trip was creating. The word had been passed down the line, and the reception accorded at Champaign was like an ovation. And the receptions were repeated at each successive freight division point—after Champaign, Centralia—then Carbondale—then Mounds—then out of the corn region and into the cotton belt to Jackson, in Tennessee,—and at last Water Valley, Mississippi.

Never had there been anything like the run of the 638.

Steaming pompously out of the cities and towns and gliding gaily through the open country, went the 638, while her proud young runner took occasion to display his skill with the whistle, an instrument of a single note, only, but under the magic touch of Casey Jones capable of producing an indescribably fascinating sound; a sound so entirely identified with Casey himself that it was recognized throughout the countryside the instant its faintest far-away sound struck upon the ear. None other could reproduce the peculiarity of that whistle song. No other sound could so arouse the interest of the grown-ups and excite the imagination of the children and the darkies.

Between stops, Casey delighted, also, to lean out of the cab window in characteristic pose and watch the dizzy dance of the heavy connecting rods and the spin of the huge drivers of this new giant of the rails. To him everything of Power and Progress that the railroad stood for was symbolized by those rapidly revolving wheels. Massive, irresistible in their onward rush, they typified the Spirit of the American Railroad.

No wonder wives and sweethearts felt twinges of jealousy! Here was a distraction to which they were extremely sensitive, but seldom understood.—Just *why* did the men bestow upon their engines feminine names, ascribe to them all sorts of virtues and refer to them in such terms of endearment? Even Janie was susceptible at times to this emotion.

Past a cotton field, through the cut and into the outskirts of the little city of Water Valley rolled the 638. The yards were crowded with folks waiting to welcome Casey Jones. The fireboy on the last lap rose to the occasion and showed what he could do with the bell.

He yelled across to his engineer: "Watch, Mr. Casey!"

Casey nodded approvingly.

"I been watching," he shouted back. "She always stops on the upright and never turns over. I couldn't do any better myself."

Now and then the bell, gleaming brightly, stopped in upright position, not swinging back until the motion of the engine jarred it loose. A practised hand was required to manipulate it so well, and the resultant slow, stately tolling of the bell lent additional dignity to the arrival of the 638.

First off, Casey espied Janie among the crowd. He swept her up from the cinders in a hearty bear hug and across her shoulder encountered the contemplative gaze of George Dickey, his master mechanic.

He eased Janie to the ground and spoke cheerfully to the master mechanic.

"Looks like you got something for me, Governor."

The M. M. stepped up, shook hands and smiled.

"Take your time, Casey. No hurry right now. Just come by the office later." He glanced around over the crowd. "By the way, some of your family has come down to Water Vally to meet you."

"Eugene!" exclaimed Casey, sighting his brother. Eugene was studiously inspecting No. 638, not paying any immediate attention to Casey.

Casey strode over to him.

"Hey, Bud," he said, "look around here."

Eugene, his face alight with a grin, looked around.

"Remember what I told you way back yonder?" Casey said meaningly.

"Think I can remember all the crazy things you told me?" retorted Eugene.

"You'll remember this," said Casey. And he deliberately knocked his brother's hat from his head.

An angry light flashed in Eugene's eyes. Then he suddenly remembered.

"Durn your old hide!" he exclaimed. "When you left Cayce you said you'd do that some day."

He picked up his hat from the cinders. Now he doffed it and bowed low to 638.

"Buddy," he turned to the smiling Casey, grasping his hand, "you're an honor to the Illinois Central—and the Jones family. I'm sure proud of you, old man."

Casey's look fell upon a ragged and dirty little Negro who was standing in the forefront of a number of others of his race.

"Wallace!"

Wallace's joy was unmistakable. People turned to look at the little darky.

"Yassuh, Mist' Casey," replied Wallace. He waved a hand toward the other Negroes, all grinning fatuously. "Mos' o' dese boys come down on a wuk train to see you an' yo' new engine."

"That's fine!" said Casey heartily, really meaning it. "You having any more bad dreams?"

Wallace suddenly sobered.

"Yassuh, Mist' Casey. Us had dat dream agin."

"What?" exclaimed Casey. "The bale of hay—shelled corn—and all?"

Wallace's expression showed that he was sorely troubled. "Yassuh. Twicet I dreamt hit. Come us dream hit agin it gwinter mean sumpin'."

Casey gave Wallace a pat on the back that nearly upset him. He laughed happily, turning again to Janie but calling to the Negro.

"Boy, you leave that cheap gin alone!"

CHAPTER XXXII

ROUNDHOUSE CHAT

AT THE roundhouse office, Master Mechanic Dickey listened with lively interest to what Casey had to say about the initial run of the 638.

"I know you had a scrumptious time, Casey, you old hogger. Never heard of a run like that," complimented the M. M. "By the way, what you going to do with all the glad rags on your new baby?"

"You can have 'em for the kids, Governor," replied Casey. "From now on everybody from Kingdom Come will know the 638 by her whippoorwill call."

"Thanks," said the M. M., acknowledging the gift, "I'll take 'em home to the children before you check out on your next run."

"Only one thing lacking on the trip down," Casey reverted to his favorite theme of the moment, "if I'd only had about twenty-five loaded cars——"

"What do you mean, twenty-five loaded cars?" interrupted the master mechanic. "Don't you know twenty-two is supposed to be the standard drag for the 600 class locomotive?"

"Yes, but that's foolish," returned Casey seriously, "thirty or more might not be a fair drag the way they load 'em now."

Master Mechanic Dickey slapped his knee to emphasize his forthcoming remark.

"You're right, Casey, and that's just the thing this railroad's beginning to work on now. Not much longer will a fixed maximum number of so-called loads and empties make a train; and then it won't be so easy for old Slim to flip a bag of beans in an empty, mark it a load and get away with it. Ever hear of James J. Hill?"

"Sure. He's President of the Great Northern. I hear he's always thinking up something new."

"Exactly," continued the master mechanic, "and he has the idea that a new system is needed in order to get a sure enough load out of every haul. You know each locomotive has a certain hauling capacity or tonnage rating. Well, in making up a train all cars ought to be weighed and checked and the load of the train, instead of being based on a special number of loads and empties, should be determined according to tonnage, depending on the capacity of the locomotive. The number of cars would be sort of secondary."

"Now that makes sense," said Casey with enthusiasm.

"But before finally adopting any new system the company officials are requiring tests to be made, and—" Master Mechanic Dickey arose, rubbed his hands and pursed his mouth significantly "—and this is where *you* come in, Casey my boy."

Casey grinned understandingly.

"So that's what you wanted to see me about, eh? Well, what it takes, me and 638's got!"

CHAPTER XXXIII

TONNAGE TEST

PROMPTLY at four o'clock the next morning, Casey, lamp in hand, answered the call-boy's sharp rap at the door of his room at Mrs. Block's boarding house.

"Extra north, Mr. Casey, with No. 638 at nine A.M."

"Thanks, Bud. Are you sure it's 638?"

"Sure enough, Mr. Casey," replied the boy, "and last night I heard the yardmaster and switchmen say that Casey Jones would never get that long heavy drag over Waterford without doubling."

"That's what *they* think, Bud," smiled Casey, "but don't you worry."

He closed the door softly, hoping to dress and leave the house without disturbing Janie. He was filled with consternation when he turned to find her sitting up in bed, hands over her face, weeping bitterly.

"Janie, honey, what in the world's the matter?" he cried, rushing over to her.

"I—I heard everything," she sobbed. "W—Why did they call you so early for a nine o'clock run? W—Won't they ever let you stay with me just a little while?"

"Now, honey, don't blame the railroad. I know the call ought to have been at seven o'clock, but I tipped the boy to make it early and he was on the job. You know this run is the most important I've had and I want plenty of time to check up on my 638."

"*Your* 638!" she screamed furiously, wringing her hands, "I hate your 638. You love that old engine better than you do me, and I came all the way from Jackson just to be with you! I hate the railroad! I hate you!" She turned and buried her face in the pillow, shoulders heaving in an ecstasy of emotion, half grief, half anger.

"Sugarfoots!" he remonstrated helplessly.

Casey sought in every way he knew how to soothe and placate Janie, but every effort failed and finally, his spirits somewhat dampened, he departed for the roundhouse after telling her he would see her later at home in Jackson.

"And, honey," he said before closing the door, "when you hear the whippoorwill call sounding out through Cathey's Cut and Springdale Bottom you'll know your old man's thinking of you and loves you."

Before pulling out of Water Valley on his first test run with No. 638, Casey received the good wishes of Master Mechanic Dickey and others, assuring them in return that the test was as good as made.

Realizing that Waterford Hill was the main hazard ahead, Casey had seen to it that the sand pipes were clear and everything in readiness for an emergency, although he never doubted that the 638 would make the grade.

It was a tough pull and there were many anxious moments when it looked as though the extra heavy drag would stall. Finally, when the nose of the 638 eased over the crest, Casey, now assured of success, grinned across at his fireboy and yelled:

"Ain't she sweet?"

During this period and for a number of years thereafter similar tests were made on the various districts, for example by Lee Chandler with engine No. 611 on the Cairo district, and so progressively successful were these that finally, in 1899, the Illinois Central definitely adopted the "Tonnage System," J. W. Higgins being Superintendent of Transportation at the time.

CHAPTER XXXIV

THE JONES FAMILY

UPON Casey's arrival at Jackson at the end of the test run he was called upon to double out over the Cairo district with an extra north to Mounds, Illinois, there being a shortage of engineers. Upon his return to Jackson he was given two days of much needed rest, and he decided to devote most of this time to his family and to take stock of things generally.

Janie rushed into his arms and he held her close for a long moment. The painful scene at Mrs. Block's boarding house in Water Valley was never mentioned.

"Sugarfoots," he whispered, "there'll be no call-boy disturbing us in the morning. Gosh! I'm glad to be home."

Casey had become a family man, and he was ever a devoted husband and father. The first child, Charles, was born July 15, 1888, and a daughter, Helen, was born October 10, 1890. They were now old enough to run to meet him when he came home from his runs, and he played with them and spent as much time with them as he could. John Lloyd, the third and last child, was born later, on March 27, 1896.

The two days layover enabled Casey to see his father

and mother, who in the meantime had removed to Jackson along with the three other brothers. Inasmuch as the boys were all now working on the railroad and Emma was still holding her position with Hayes-Brown Department Store, Casey no longer was called upon to contribute to their support. Furthermore, Casey's father had obtained a good position as teacher in the Medina school, near Jackson.

Eugene, who started his road career on the Cairo district of the I. C. as flagman, continued until he was promoted to conductor; then he changed to the smoke end and qualified as fireman, later being promoted to engineer and assigned to engine 606. Years after Casey's demise, Eugene was accidentally shot and killed in Ft. Worth, Texas.

Frank began in orthodox manner as fireman on the Illinois Central and later became engineer. Frank Jones was the only one of the brothers who could in any sense be called a rounder or boomer railroader. In February, 1902, the writer encountered Frank at Thistle Junction, Utah, serving with the Denver & Rio Grande Railroad as roundhouse foreman. While railroading in the west, Frank was sometimes called "Casey," confusing him with his famous brother; but Casey himself was never connected with any railroad other than the Mobile & Ohio and the Illinois Central. Frank was the only one of the Jones children who died a natural death. He died in Virginia in 1919 and was buried at Corona, Alabama.

From engine caller Phillip, youngest of the boys, also became an engineer on the Illinois Central, his chief ambition being to become as great a hoghead as brother Casey. Phillip most resembled Casey—size, appearance, character and disposition.

Phillip met his death on a Mounds to Memphis run in 1921 near Arlington, Kentucky. The writer was Phillip's conductor for nearly two years near the turn of the century, during which period of time they were room-mates. Phillip frequently asked the writer to run his engine while he would busy himself by walking out on the running board to oil the airpump packing,— an unnecessarily hazardous undertaking which had become a habit with him, and against which the writer often warned him. He was thus engaged when an airhose burst, suddenly checking the speed of the train and throwing him off the locomotive. His remains were carried to a blacksmith shop and later picked up by engineer Colie Chandler and others.

During the two days rest period at Jackson, Casey and Janie called especially to see Ann Nolen Jones. Casey, knowing his mother's persistent lack of enthusiasm for the railroad, decided to let her do most of the talking.

"You know I'm proud of you, son," said his mother, fondly, "I've watched your progress all these years on your beloved railroad. Now we all seem to be getting along very well, even if Emma does stay away too much with her work and her friends. But somehow I don't like to think of the future. I like to look back when you were a little boy. After all, you're still a child in lots of ways." She smiled at Janie, who nodded emphatically.

"I can see you now," continued Ann Nolen Jones, reminiscently, "leaving Cayce with your shiny patent-leather valise, all excited and hopeful of the future." She sighed. "I knew you had your own life to live, and you've done well, but you'll always be to me the Luther of the days before the railroad got you."

Casey kissed his mother affectionately.

"I know one thing," he said with emotion, "I've got the sweetest, finest mother in the world!"

"And the finest father, too," reminded Ann Nolen. "Think of him out there teaching this very minute. And don't forget the other children, how wonderful they are."

"Right you are, mother," agreed Casey, then he sobered. "By the way I've sure got to drop by and see Emma before I start on my run."

More than ever Casey was impressed by Emma's good looks and high spirits, but it was all very disturbing to him. He attempted to upbraid her for not spending more time at home, but she wouldn't let him finish.

"Casey, you're so funny and old-fashioned."

"I reckon I love you so much, Sis, I can't help being funny," he chided.

CHAPTER XXXV

THE RESCUE

IT WAS four o'clock the next morning when the call-boy knocked.

"Fifth No. 81 for six o'clock, Mr. Casey Jones." It was a high piping voice, but curiously fresh and musical.

"You mean *638* for fifth No. 81, don't you, Mickey, my boy?" Casey opened the door.

"'Course, Mr. Casey," protested Mickey, flashing a smile through the semi-darkness. "The brass hats wouldn't let any other hogger run that engine. Lot's o' rails say No. 638 is your engine sure 'nuff. Mr. Colie Chandler says so."

"You mean Mr. *Runt* Chandler." Casey remembered that Colie had pulled in at midnight with Lee hauling a coal drag. "I'll bet a quarter, Mickey, against the one I just gave you that Mr. Runt Chandler hasn't been home since he arrived in Chester Street yard."

Mickey shook his head owlishly.

"Naw, sir, you won't. 'Cause I heard Mr. Colie say he was goin' over to Tomlin's Hall and take those poor bastards off the south end for a good ride. Th' paycar run late yesterday, and he thought pickins ud be easy."

The paymaster was S. H. Charles who knew every employee on the road. When passing a pay envelope to Runt Chandler he always advised him to "look out for loaded dice."

It was the custom for train and engine crews receiving early morning calls to stop in at the Blue Front restaurant, a greasy spoon near the yard, and get on the outside of a stack of flapjacks with bacon and eggs sunny side up. Here Casey met his conductor, old Bob Stevenson, who had arrived early and had already checked his train—every car loaded with wheat for New Orleans and export.

Stevenson exhibited his waybills and commented on the heavy train put together by the yard crew—Ruddy Hays, Walter Cisco, Marion Stewart and Charlie Schmuck. Casey had not seen any of these men in the restaurant, but when it was nearly time to leave he espied Ruddy in the corner watching him covertly from the corner of one roguish eye. The look was enough for the engineer.

As they were about to leave, the door swung open and Runt Chandler sauntered in, looking a bit red-eyed and disheveled, but talkative as usual.

"Hello, you old Jack Driver. You boys holdin' a convention?"

"Nope," responded Casey, easily. "We're waitin' for Kit Scruggs and his horse-car to come take us down to th' roundhouse. Which reminds me, Runt. How long you been in? Are you goin' out on a extra north?"

"Me?" parried Runt, settling himself at the counter and signalling for the inevitable flapjacks and accessories. "Why, me, I jus' got in. Been doin' a little work on Lee's six eleven."

"Sure it wasn't *seven eleven?* I can make 638 climb a tree any day, but I never knew a Chandler could drive a engine up over Tomlin's Hall."

Runt shrugged his shoulders with an air of resignation and spoke feelingly between mouthfuls of flapjacks.

"Yeah, they cleaned me good.—But you jus' wait.— I'll take them mugs for a ride yet.—How 'bout lettin' me have four bits?"

Casey walked down the yard alongside his train, carefully giving it the once over. Yes, that bunch of roughnecks had tried to slip something over.—Bolivar Hill, near the town of Bolivar, Tennessee, was the steepest grade between Jackson and Water Valley, and the yard crew, having heard much of the successful tonnage tests, had added three extra cars to an already heavy drag in the hope that Casey would be compelled to double. But would he double Bolivar Hill? Never!

This resolve prompted him to do something that perhaps had never been undertaken by any other engineer,—an act constituting a dischargeable offense. The steam gauges for the six hundred class engines were set at 165 and 175 pounds, and engineers dared not tamper with these devices. But the venturesome Casey took a chance by screwing down the pop valve, and while the gauge registered 175 pounds his engine was actually carrying 195 pounds of steam, or twenty pounds excess. He was determined to make Bolivar Hill, come Hell or High Water!

Fifth No. 81 was well on its way south when old Bob Stevenson, having made out his wheel report and with nothing else to do, decided to walk over the fast moving train to the engine cab where he was warmly greeted.

"Hi, fella. You're now ridin' the best engine on this man's railroad. Jus' stick your head out th' cab window, Bud, and watch them drivers roll. Ain't she sweet?"

"Yeah," came the mocking retort, "but just you wait 'til she sticks her nose up the hill. That's why I'm here. I've already told the flagman to anchor the rear end down soon's we stall and beat it back 99 telegraph poles while we take over the head end."

"Like Hell, you did! This baby'll never stall, Uncle Bob.—Not 638."

Up Bolivar Hill creeped the locomotive, exhausts farther and farther apart and each seemingly the last, —a huge palpitating monster struggling for the precious breath that would mean the difference between life and death. Her driver talked to her in affectionate tones.

"Good old gal! You know you can make it. Don't fail me now!" And he slapped the outside of the cab with his open hand in exhortation and encouragement.

"I'll bet five dollars we double," cried Bob Stevenson. "We'll never make it."

"All right, Bud," Casey flung back over his shoulder. "I'll take that bet, and my name's not Runt Chandler either. This is one time your Uncle'll be ahead o' th' game, by th' Eternal!"

Another agonizing hundred yards of almost imperceptible progress, and the nose of No. 638 barely eased over the crest of the grade, while her driver let out an Indian yell and reached for the whistle cord. Out across the hillsides and valleys sounded the familiar whippoorwill call.

The meddling with the pop valve had produced results. The secret was later divulged by Phillip Jones, who never tried his brother's risky scheme.

Ahead of them lay Grand Junction where they found a red board and an order to pick up two cars of live stock at Holly Springs which had been placed on the interchange track by the K.C.M. & B. Ry., destined New Orleans. Bob Stevenson, not feeling any too good over the loss of five bucks, spoke glumly.

"Why the Hell didn't they have the Irish Mail do this pick up work?"

But his engineer was in a cheerful, bantering mood.

"Are you askin' me, fella? Or should I wire W. S. King, our Superintendent at Jackson? You know, Bud, there's one King can trump a Ace, and you better think twice before callin' his hand."

Bob Stevenson looked his disgust but offered no

denial of Casey's last assertion. In truth, there was not an employee on the division who would dare presume upon the Superintendent or fail to carry out his orders to the letter. Rails will recall a sign placed on the lawn in front of the Division Building at Jackson which read "Keep off the Grass"—an injunction that was strictly obeyed.

The chatter continued until they approached Michigan City, Mississippi, when the young engineer, unable to keep still, asked Stevenson to run the engine while he walked out on the running board to oil the relief valves. This quickly done, he advanced from the running board to the steam chest and thence to the pilot beam to adjust the spark screen,—which operation he hoped to complete and make his way back to the cab before arriving in town.

Stevenson had reduced the speed by making a service application with the air brakes, a process with which he was not entirely familiar. As Casey started to retrace his steps to the cab he noted absently that they were passing a string of cars stored on a siding. Suddenly he saw a group of small children dash from the blind side in front of a gondola some sixty yards ahead and proceed directly across the main line in front of the oncoming train. It seemed that all the careless youngsters would make it safely across but all at once a tiny girl in the rear of the group stopped squarely between the rails and stood frozen in her tracks, facing the approaching locomotive.

Rescue

"My God! Steve—Bob, reverse!" yelled Casey,
while almost in the same breath he cried to the little girl,
"Get off, honey, quick! Get off!"

Then, realizing that the youngster was completely
paralyzed by fear and could not move, he went into
action. In one continuous movement he stepped
quickly to the tip of the pilot or cowcatcher and crouched
in position for the inevitable impact, noting that the
speed of the train had been only slightly retarded.

As the wild-eyed, terror-stricken little figure loomed
directly in front of him, Casey, timing himself for a
mighty effort, reached far out and down and swept her
safely into the hollow of his long arm.

"Thank God," he breathed.

The train came to a stop and Casey stepped to the
ground, the rescued child held tightly in both arms.
Stevenson, pale of face, came running up and the children gathered around joyfully, while Casey sought to
engage the little girl in conversation. Her feet had
barely grazed the surface of the cowcatcher and he
knew she was not hurt, but he wanted to make sure she
was sufficiently recovered from fright before sending
her home and warning her to stay off the railroad
tracks. Much as he wished to do so, he did not have
time to take her to her home.

The tiny, delicate little figure clung to him for a
long moment, but finally she looked into his face,
smiled and thanked him. Reluctantly he put her down

and she started home in company with the other children.

"What a sweet, pretty child," said Casey, looking after her fondly. "Reminds me of my little Helen. Just about her age."

CHAPTER XXXVI

LITTLE GENEVA

UPON returning to Jackson, Casey made out his usual work report and stopped in at the Blue Front, seated himself at the counter, and placed an order for T-bone steak, french fried potatoes and cream gravy. The near tragedy at Michigan City had sobered him considerably, and he experienced vague pricklings of a suddenly disturbed conscience. He had advised an innocent little girl to be careful, while he himself, although possessed of a superior understanding of the mechanics and the limitations of a railroad locomotive, had deliberately violated one of the company's strictest rules. Painstaking and cautious according to his own standards, he knew he could not resist doing things that others might regard as foolhardy; all because he wanted to be preeminent in his chosen field.

Thus absorbed in his own reflections, he did not observe the presence of the yard crew until he heard the bantering voice of Marion Stewart.

"Gee, how youse guys can put away the groceries!"

Casey's reply was accompanied by a meaning glance at Ruddy Hays, who squirmed uncomfortably.

"Why, fellas, this is th' way to keep fit so's you can get over Bolivar without doubling."

Casey strolled leisurely homeward. He planned to enter the house and get to bed without disturbing the household. But Janie met him at the door.

"Your breakfast's ready, dear. I knew you'd be here soon when I heard you coming through Forked Deer bottoms."

He kissed her.

"You're mighty sweet, honey, but I done had me a big T-bone steak down at the Blue Front, and I'm ready to hit th' hay."

"Casey Jones, you need killing! Don't you know this is Friday? If you keep on eating red meats you'll be moping around with high blood pressure."

"By George, Sugarfoots, I plum forgot it's Friday. I'm sorry."

"And you're not going to bed either," Janie concluded, dramatically. "The call-boy's looking for you now to double out on an extra south."

Extra 638 with a coal drag pulled out of Chester Street yard, Jackson, Tennessee, for Water Valley, closely trailing a second class freight loaded with perishables. A short distance south of Michigan City No. 638 was stopped by the flagman of the preceding train who stated that about a third of his train was in the ditch and the main line completely blocked. Casey, after taking the required precautions, backed his train into Michigan City and reported the wreck, whereupon wrecking crews were ordered from Jackson and Water Valley.

During the intervening hours required to clear the line Casey wandered in characteristic manner through the little village, visiting old friends and making new ones. Mrs. Ned Brownlow, wife of a section foreman who was well-known to the engineer, was the first to invite him to supper, the evening meal, and he readily accepted.

As they approached the Brownlow residence a small girl jumped off the front porch and came running directly to Casey whom she grasped around the knee.

"Geneva!" cried Mrs. Brownlow in surprise, and then to Casey: "This is our little daughter, Mr. Jones, I don't believe you've ever seen her. I never saw her act this way."

Casey reached down, picked up the child and smiled archly into her bright little face.

"Who's this ugly old man, honey?" he asked.

"My great, big engineer man!"

Thus did the astonished Mrs. Brownlow learn the identity of the trainman who saved her child's life. Nor had Casey previously known whose child he had rescued.

Upon returning to Jackson he had Janie purchase a pretty doll and dress it up for little Geneva. It was given her for a Christmas present, and she named it "Casey Jones."

CHAPTER XXXVII

THE DINNER PARTY

THE dinner party in honor of Casey Jones was held at the old Southern Hotel facing Court Square in Jackson, Tennessee, and came as a complete surprise to that distinguished young rail. A semi-formal affair, it was given in the early spring of 1896 and was the result of weeks of secret planning on the part of a group of relatives and friends, including Mrs. Day, the beloved owner and manager of the popular cosmopolitan hotel on the site of which now stands the palatial, air-conditioned *New Southern Hotel* with its two hundred and fifty rooms and every modern convenience,— an accepted center of social and civic activity in the thriving Hub City of West Tennessee.

In the days preceding the big event so great was the demand for articles of dress and apparel, both substantial and superficial, that stores such as G. H. Robertson & Co., specializing in exclusive mens' wear, and Hayes-Brown, Sol Tuchfeld and others, including the three-ball hock shops, did a surprisingly thriving business. Formal and informal suits of various design, articles such as large puff ties, high stiff linen and celluloid collars, long toothpick shoes of the Stacy-Adams and Edwin Clapp brands with spats, the popular John B.

wrecking crews were ordered from Jackson and Water Valley.

During the intervening hours required to clear the line Casey wandered in characteristic manner through the little village, visiting old friends and making new ones. Mrs. Ned Brownlow, wife of a section foreman who was well-known to the engineer, was the first to invite him to supper, the evening meal, and he readily accepted.

As they approached the Brownlow residence a small girl jumped off the front porch and came running directly to Casey whom she grasped around the knee.

"Geneva!" cried Mrs. Brownlow in surprise, and then to Casey: "This is our little daughter, Mr. Jones, I don't believe you've ever seen her. I never saw her act this way."

Casey reached down, picked up the child and smiled archly into her bright little face.

"Who's this ugly old man, honey?" he asked.

"My great, big engineer man!"

Thus did the astonished Mrs. Brownlow learn the identity of the trainman who saved her child's life. Nor had Casey previously known whose child he had rescued.

Upon returning to Jackson he had Janie purchase a pretty doll and dress it up for little Geneva. It was given her for a Christmas present, and she named it "Casey Jones."

COLIE CHANDLER

Illinois Central engineer who, strangely moved by a premonition that Casey Jones was going to his death when he accepted the Cannonball Express run, was the last person to tell Casey good-bye.

In order to permit the attendance of Casey's closest friends of the railroad, every available extra man was pressed into service; and invitations were extended by the invitation committee to numerous officials of both the Illinois Central and Mobile & Ohio as well as to a number of prominent citizens of Jackson and surrounding territory not connected with the railroad.

Among well-known railroaders invited were Jake Neudorfer, in later years City Councilman of Jackson; Dave Staley; Dick Clark; John Baxter; Major E. S. Hosford; the Chandlers; the Gaffneys; Tom Weldon; Charlie Schmuck; Ed Rarick; Dixie Fenner; Lee Merritt; William Hatfield; Billy Sheehan; W. S. King; W. G. Eby;—and, of course, their wives and sweethearts.

The crowd were assembled in their respective places in the beautifully decorated dining hall and Toastmaster Colie (Runt) Chandler, in formal attire, stood in position at the head table to formally proclaim the opening of the party. On the table in front of him was a huge brass bell gleaming resplendently in the light of the bright gas chandeliers suspended from the ceiling. At the sound of the gong a hush fell over the assembly and they were asked to stand while the Reverend George Tucker, evangelist and engineer, invoked the blessings of God. Their seats resumed, they listened to the clear, vibrant voice of Runt Chandler.

"Ladies and Gentlemen, we're gathered here this evenin' to honor a man who deserves it, and we're goin' to have a good time. We know what sort of a fella he is. There never was a harder worker, a more loyal friend or a better citizen. Of course he's been honored by others who don't know him or love him near as much as we do, so we thought it was high time to get together and show him what we think of him. There's those here tonight who can sing his praises better than I can, and they'll be called on later, but since I'm specially honored by bein' toastmaster I had to say a few words before we go ahead with the eats. You know who I'm talkin' about, folks. He's sittin' here to my right between me and his charmin' wife, and I'm goin' to ask him to stand up and make a bow at this time. Ladies and Gentlemen, Casey Jones."

They were all on their feet cheering and applauding as the embarrassed young giant stood red-faced and smiling before them.

It was a noisy, happy gathering and they enjoyed an excellent meal of the Old South. And none enjoyed it more thoroughly than Casey himself. He later described the evening as the climax of the happiest period of his life, the years 1893–1896.

Colie Chandler resumed.

"Ladies and Gentlemen, I'm about to call on a man who did a whole lot to make Casey Jones the great railroader he is today: I take pleasure in introducin' our friend Bose Lashley."

"Ladies and Gentlemen." Lashley's voice had a soft, pleasing quality. "This is the first time I ever tried to make a speech in my life, and you couldn't lift me to my feet with a derrick if it wasn't for the fact I'm called on to say somethin' about a boy I love like a brother.

"Let me say right here that Casey Jones deserves every honor you can give him. I know. When he was just gettin' to be a cub operator I named him "Casey," and later on I introduced him to his wife. He was my fireman on many a run, and when Mary Ellen and me was on our honeymoon we witnessed his baptism down in Whistler, Alabama. I saw his loyalty to a friend when he resented with mighty force the threats and insults of a big bully, and I know he stands for what's right and just. He's a great railroader and a real man. Folks, you've done a fine thing in givin' this party for my friend, Casey, and I'm mighty proud to be here."

Spontaneous applause followed the earnest words of Bose Lashley.

Toastmaster Chandler then introduced Major E. S. Hosford. Deep silence prevailed as the guests awaited the words of this highly respected official who was known to have played an important part in the career of the young man they were honoring. Surely this must be the climax of the program.

The Major was a man of fine bearing and he spoke with dignity and precision.

"Mr. Toastmaster, Guests and Friends, this is an occasion of exceeding joy to me. As a railroad executive of many years service, I credit myself with one special talent. That is the ability to judge men.

"Mingling here tonight with this fine crowd of people and listening to the remarks that have been made, I feel that this party is really a testimonial to my own good judgment. At any rate, permit me to indulge this happy thought while I briefly review the years since the time I saw a long, gangling youth of barely fifteen years demonstrate on the sandlot of Cayce, Kentucky, remarkable ability as a baseball player and a true sense of good sportsmanship. He played the game hard, but never would he take an unfair advantage.

"This youngster presented himself at Columbus, Kentucky, looking for a job at a time when I happened to be there. He was spurred on by a grim determination and was ably supported by our friend Lashley. It was my pleasure to give encouragement to his ambition and he became a cub operator. Since then I have followed almost every move of his career. I know what he has accomplished as a railroader and I know many other fine things about him that he himself would never mention. Of course he admits he's a great engineer and even boasts of it in the good-natured way of all born railroaders, but at heart he's the most modest of men.

"While he is still a young man in his prime, it is fitting that we should pay him in some small measure the sort of honor all too frequently reserved for those heroes who have since passed on to the Great Beyond.

"Show me the boy who perhaps in the shortest time on record became an accomplished telegraph operator, and I want to praise him while he can hear my voice. Show me the man who is always kind and friendly, honest and true, and I want to commend him to his face. Show me the man who by his natural charm and personality commands the instinctive admiration and affection of little children and the veneration of the darkeys, and I want to tell the world that there is a character worth while. Show me the man talented far beyond the average who yet retains the affectionate regard of his fellow workers, and I'll show you a man who deserves every living evidence of that esteem. Show me the man who time and again has shown his willingness to give his life for another, and I'll show you a man who ought to be placed upon a living pedestal.

"So, my friends, we honor Casey Jones, not merely for what he's done, but for the kind of man he is.

> " 'We do well who tribute pay
>   To him who loves and lives today.' "

Colie Chandler stood gulping and blinking while the applause gradually subsided. He waited until the flurry of small white lace-bordered handkerchiefs was superseded by an occasional sniff, and then he spoke.

"Thank you, Major Hosford, that was the greatest

speech I ever heard and I know we'll all remember it
as long as we live. By the way, folks, I almost forgot
to thank you-all for everything you did to make this
party possible. Everybody did his part and it's a great
success. I especially want to thank my dear brother
Lee, who was so kind as to lend this beautiful bell off
his engine No. 611 for us to use as a dinner gong.
Somehow he's been pretty close to Casey and I'm going
to call on him now. I know you're goin' to hear another great speech. All right, Lee, let's have it."

Lee Chandler struggled to his feet and began fum-
bling through his pockets for something that apparently
was missing. Finally he abandoned the futile effort,
buttoned his coat, grasped the top rung of his chair
tightly in both hands, cleared his throat and blurted
out:

"Ladies and Gentlemen, I ask you what would you
do if you had a smart alec brother who stole your bell,
swiped your speech and then called on you to follow
a great man like Major Hosford? I ask you, what
would you do?—Well that's exactly what *I'm* goin' to
do—later. Folks, I don't know if there's anything
new I can say about Casey, except I know he's the best
scout that ever was and the hardest drivin' hoghead
that ever pulled a throttle. I'm mighty proud to call
him my friend."

Runt Chandler's face bore a look of amused innocence.

"Now, Ladies and Gentlemen, after that brilliant

effort by my elder brother we'll have a few words from Casey and then we'll all ramble up to Tomlin's Hall and dance 'til the roosters start crowin'. All right, old timer. Tell us about it."

Never was the imposing figure and tremendous personality of Casey Jones so apparent as at that moment. Filled with emotion almost beyond expression, he stood in silent contemplation of these warm hearted friends, his dark, glowing eyes picking out one and then another with a look of understanding and affection. Then he turned and took Janie by the arm, drawing her to her feet by his side.

"Friends, you've made me the happiest man in the world tonight, and I want to thank you from the bottom of my heart."

The dance at Tomlin's Hall was in every way typical of the gay nineties, a combination of comical formality and hysterical sociability. It lingers among the happy memories of many old-timers.

The music was provided by a local band and special entertainers were brought in from Memphis. Across the hall opposite the entrance was a long counter where strawberry, sarsaparilla and cherry soda pop, supplemented by a large tub of pink lemonade, were ready to be dispensed by white-aproned black boys to those who desired that kind of refreshment. Later in the night, between dances, the ladies and some of the men gathered here in gossipy groups, but there were those who kept the trail hot between the dance hall and Bell's

saloon for other sorts of beverage, such as Taylor &
Williams' Yellowstone and Kentucky Turf.

The band went to work in earnest and repeatedly
struck up the ever popular numbers *After The Ball*,
In The Shade Of The Old Apple Tree, *The Blue
Danube* and *The Good Old Summer Time*, occasionally
drifting off into livelier tunes of a different tempo in
order to accommodate the square dance, Virginia Reel,
schottische and cake walk.

During the early part of the first intermission the
amateurs took over and two male quartets swung into
competitive action. The engineers composed of Ed
Rarick, S. S. Wooley, Tom Weldon and Bose Lashley
harmonized on *A Bird In A Gilded Cage* and sought
to outdo the conductors, Jim Northcott, Jim Michael,
Bob Kennedy and Cocky Blackman, who sang *A Passing
Policeman Found A Little Child*. It was very touch-
ing.

Colie Chandler then cake walked to the center of the
floor, holding aloft a pop bottle half filled with a for-
eign substance.

"Aw right, folks, le's have a li'l toast:

> *Here's to engine 638*
> *She's comin' with a whoop*
> *With Casey at th' throttle*
> *An' Johnny at th' scoop.*"

This part of the program was concluded on a plane
highly pleasing to Casey when Lee Chandler led the

ensemble in a boisterous rendition of *The Flight Of The Irish Mail*.

The entertainers from Memphis were professional vaudeville performers consisting of two frumpily dressed men and a buxom girl clad in white silk tights who called themselves the Bluff City Trio. These now came upon the scene with their crude jokes, bantering conversation, acrobatics and sleight of hand.

Then dancing was resumed.

One of the most attractive figures, and certainly the most strikingly gowned, was Casey's own sister Emma, who obviously was having a marvelous time. Her escort was a foppish young salesman from Chicago named Vincent Hatcher. Every now and then throughout the dance she would run up to Casey to make some jocular remark or give him an affectionate pat. Casey, who really enjoyed dancing, waltzed with her several times, and they presented a handsome picture.

Emma's costume was the last word in formal evening wear. Her gown was an elaborate creation consisting of a combination of carmine taffeta skirt and separate flesh colored lace bodice. The skirt was very full, falling in a train in the back. A knife-pleated taffeta drop petticoat rustled and swished as she danced. The lace bodice had the wasp waist of the era with a low heart-shaped neckline, taffeta peplum and large puffed sleeves, their bouffant appearance increased by crinoline plumpers. The sleeves ended at the elbow with lace ruffles, meeting the elbow-length glace kid gloves. Her blue-black hair was done high on her head and topped by a perfect Psyche knot and brilliant crimson ornament. Comments were favorable and otherwise, but none could dispute her beauty.

At the refreshment counter Casey ordered a bottle of pop for Emma. He had wanted to talk with her apart from others.

"All right, Snow Ball, hand up a bottle o' cherry pop."

"Yas, suh, Mist' Casey." That voice!

"Wallace!" Casey was both surprised and pleased. "First one place and then another. Boy, what you doin' here?"

"Us heerd some mens down in Canton talk 'bout dis party, Mist' Casey, and us jus' had to come see you, suh!"

"That's fine." Casey laughed, then seriously: "You been havin' any more of them dreams about baled hay and shelled corn?"

"Not 'zactly, suh." Wallace's wizened countenance bore a curiously troubled expression. "Dis time us done dreamed 'bout a big rivah, an' a big boat an' a big storm."

"Wallace, I been tellin' you to leave that nigger gin alone. Here take this so when you deadhead back you'll have a little extra on th' side. Maybe I'll see you again soon." Casey slipped the little darkey a five dollar bill, took Emma's arm and walked with her across the hall where they seated themselves.

"What that little negro said about the river made me feel queer." Emma's fingers fluttered about her throat. Her face had lost its vivid color.

"I know, Sis, but jus' try and forget it. Wallace always has funny dreams." Casey took her hand and continued wistfully: "Honey, you know I want you to be happy. All this fast livin' an' these fancy clothes may be all right in a way. But somehow I always like to think of you as th' little girl back there in Cayce, like when we kissed each other goodbye when I started off to Columbus."

The simple child-like glow of love in her dark eyes at that sincere moment years ago outshone the fire of living that lighted them afterwards.

CHAPTER XXXVIII

EMMA'S DEATH

IT WAS two-thirty o'clock on the morning of May 27, 1896, that Casey, running 638 south, stopped at Holly Springs, Mississippi. A man, catching the gangway step, pulled himself up into the cab, and Casey recognized Engineer John Baxter. Baxter was in work clothes and from the manner in which he invaded the cab it was apparent that he was taking possession.

"All right, Casey old boy," were Baxter's first words. "You can hop the extra-north I just brought in. I'll get your drag to Water Valley."

Casey stared.

"What you talking about, Baxter?" he exclaimed. Then a fearful thought flashed into his mind and he asked quietly: "Anything happened?"

Baxter started to reply. "There ought to be somethin' here for you," he began, but was interrupted by the telegraph operator who handed up a message.

Casey's first glance took in the signature of his trainmaster. Then he read:

STEAMBOAT KATHLEEN SUNK OFF BIRDSPOINT YESTERDAY. EMMA AMONG LIST OF DROWNED.

Casey read the words over and over again, as though he could not comprehend their meaning. As the message blurred before his vision, he raised his head and stood gazing into empty space, untold anguish reflected in every feature. He seemed to be staring into infinity. Then his eyes closed and he murmured:

"Is that what th' poor little girl saw out there in th' river?"

He climbed down out of the cab and walked listlessly toward the extra-north, while Baxter shook his head in helpless sympathy.

Janie, watching for him, saw his pathetic figure coming up the walk and rushed to meet him.

"Casey, darling!"

Only five of sixteen persons aboard the ill-fated *Kathleen* survived the disaster. Captain John S. Hacker, master of the Kathleen and one of the survivors, was living at Cairo, Illinois, in 1933.

The death of his only sister so affected Casey that he asked and received an extended leave of absence, during which he traveled the entire length and breadth of the Illinois Central system, including a trip from Louisville to Memphis over the C. O. & S. W.—a line recently acquired by the Illinois Central looking forward to the establishment of the main trunkline, Chicago to New Orleans, via Fulton and Memphis. That portion of this newly acquired line between Fulton and Memphis was then commonly called "The Narrow

Escape," due to the hazardous condition of the track, a condition which existed until the I. C. practically rebuilt the road by laying heavier steel on three feet of ballast.

Casey's apathy was partially dispelled by what he saw along the route from Fulton to Memphis. Work trains by the dozen; track laborers by the hundreds brought in from Louisville, Chicago, New Orleans and elsewhere; new yards at Fulton, Memphis and intermediate points. Today this stretch of road constitutes a portion of the line over which runs the crack all-Pullman, extra-fare Panama Limited, Chicago-New Orleans, with Paul Chandler alternating at the throttle.

The young engineer experienced a quickened sense of interest and pride in what his railroad was accomplishing; but the burden of his bereavement was constantly recurring and depressing his spirits. He *must* overcome this feeling somehow.

At New Orleans, throwing off an insufferable lethargy, he visited the modern docks and warehouses and this revived his spirits considerably, again reminding him of the powerful force and influence of the railroad in the progress and development of the country.

There was one person in New Orleans he had to see before leaving the Louisiana metropolis. That was Charley Spencer, whom he located at the Levee Yard office busily engaged at his desk. Casey pulled his hat brim low over his eyes and leaned across the register counter.

"Don't strain yourself, Bud."

Spencer looked up, startled. Then his homely face broke into a wide smile of welcome, and he came forward with extended hand.

"Casey Jones! You celebrated old hogger, you. Boy, but I'm glad to see you. Haven't laid eyes on you since I borrowed your valise back in Columbus. How long you going to be in New Orleans?"

Casey warmed to this welcome. It was good to see this old friend again.

"Oh, two or three days maybe. I've heard you're gettin' along fine, Charley, got a big family and made up with th' in-laws 'n' everything. When you get through with those switch lists I want you to come have dinner with me and we can talk it all over."

So at the old Poydras Market they talked it over.

CHAPTER XXXIX

638 AT BURNSIDE

IT WAS April, 1898. Engine No. 638 was in her fifth year of service without ever having been in the shops for a general overhauling. Notwithstanding the heavy and intensive service to which she had been subjected, she was still in fair condition due to the tender ministrations of her overlord. But the General Superintendent of Motive Power had instructed the Master Mechanic at Water Valley to see that the prize locomotive was in Burnside Shops for general repairs not later than May first. During the summer months it was imperative that the locomotives and rolling stock be placed in prime condition for the fall grain rush.

Casey Jones had grown more and more attached to his celebrated engine and had looked forward with dread to the time of separation from her. So when the day approached for 638 to go to Burnside Shops he was much dispirited. He confided his feelings to Master Mechanic Losey at Water Valley, stating that he felt he would never get her back again if she got that far away from him.

"You know, Mr. Losey, me and 638's been pals a long time."

The Master Mechanic was sympathetic.

"Yes, Casey, we all know how you feel, but orders are orders. I suppose you'd like to be up there and supervise the job?"

"That's just what I want to do! If they'll let me drive her to Chicago it won't cost the company a thin dime while I'm there."

A few days later the Master Mechanic handed him the following official document:

> Water Valley, Miss., April 19th, 1898.
>
> Mr. J. L. Jones,
> Engineer Engine #638.
>
> Dear Sir:
>
> This will be your authority to run Engine #638 from Water Valley, Miss., to Burnside Shops for general repairs.
>
> Yours truly,
>
> F. C. Losey,
> Master Mechanic.

On this trip 638 hauled a long banana train from Water Valley to Twenty-seventh Street, Chicago. Janie went along and a good vacation grew out of the trip.

CHAPTER XL

AMBITION ATTAINED

THERE was keen competition among rail lines of the South in bidding for the southern mail contract, and speed was a determining factor in the ultimate award to the Illinois Central. Preliminary to the award, test runs between Chicago and New Orleans were conducted over a period of thirty days. The result was the inauguration of the fastest schedules in the history of the road assigned to trains Nos. 1, 2, 3 and 4.

Engineers Dowling and Tate, on account of their seniority, were transferred from the Water Valley District and assigned to runs 1 and 4 between Memphis and Canton, a distance of 188 miles.

That portion of the track between Memphis and Grenada, Mississippi, was extremely dangerous, largely on account of the many hills and curves. It was not considered safe for trains operating at the high rate of speed required by the new schedules. The schedule of No. 1, commonly called the *Cannonball Express,* was one of the most difficult on the entire division, and it was not long until engineer Dowling met a tragic death in line of duty. A spirit of growing apprehension

Illinois Central Railroad Company

Machinery Department

Water Valley Miss, April 19th 1899

Mr. J.L.Jones,

Engineer, Engine #638

Dear Sir :-

This will be your authority to run engine #638 from Water Valley Miss. , to Burnside Shops, for General Repairs.

Yours truly,

O.F. Losey

Master Mechanic

F. C. L.

The whistle on which Casey sounded the famous whippoorwill call while running No 638.

began to manifest itself up and down the road, and speculation was rife as to who would be the next to go. A pall was cast over the entire road, especially the Water Valley District on which Dowling had served with distinction for many years.

Casey Jones learned of Dowling's death just before leaving Water Valley on a north-bound run, and the news of his friend's death affected him greatly. He knew that his seniority placed him next in line to succeed to the *Cannonball* run,—the most distinguished position that a company runner in active service could attain. But the thrill of impending realization of this ultimate ambition was naturally tempered by the thought of attaining it through the death of a friend and by the thought of having to give up his 638 forever.

At Bolivar he met engineer P. J. Gaffney who was driving engine 622. The two engineers carried on a brief conversation, the burden of which was the sad death of Engineer Dowling.

"I know it's a bad time to bring this up, Casey, old boy," said Gaffney, "but you're just as good as in Memphis. So, how about lettin' me have that whistle off 638? Let's trade right now."

"All right, Pete. I told you if I ever lost 638 I'd give you her whistle."

The exchange was made.

Upon his arrival at Jackson Casey received the expected official notification of his promotion to the *Can-*

nonball Express run between Memphis and Canton on trains Nos. 1 and 4. He returned immediately to the roundhouse lead track to bid farewell to the locomotive that had become a part of his very being. There he ran into Engineer Frank Newell, new overlord of the 638, and they silently shook hands.

On his way to the Blue Front for a cup of coffee he saw Wallace Saunders lurking in the shadows of the freight house. No longer surprised at the sudden appearances of the little engine wiper, Casey, as usual, was glad to see him and handed him a dollar. But Wallace returned it, shaking his head.

"Naw suh, Mist' Casey. Not dat dollar."

"What's th' matter, Wallace? Dreamin' again?"

"Yessuh. Us done gone an' had dat dream agin. T'ree times, Mist' Casey." Wallace was plainly troubled.

"Baled hay, shelled corn and all?" Casey persisted, curiously.

"Yessuh, Mist' Casey. Please, suh, us wants to tell you goodbye, Mist' Casey."

Casey reached out and for the first and last time shook the hand of his little black friend, and as he hurried away Wallace's soft voice floated out after him.

"Goodbye, Mist' Casey."

At the Blue Front Casey learned to his great disappointment that John Wesley McKinnie, who had fired for him for more than two years, would not be able to join him in Memphis on the *Cannonball* run due to the

MRS. CASEY JONES
A recent portrait.

objections of his family who feared for his safety. McKinnie, a bold, adventurous young rail just in his twenty-third year and a close friend and extravagant admirer of Casey Jones, had yielded with reluctance to the wishes of his people.

Janie had heard of Dowling's death and she knew that her husband would be given his run. Casey had attained a life ambition, and for his sake she was willing to give up her friends and connections in Jackson and move with the children to Memphis.—But she was strangely disturbed, and sought in vain to conceal her feelings.

It was decided that Janie and the children would not move to Memphis until she could find time to go over and locate suitable living quarters. With only two hours remaining for Casey to make a few hurried calls before the departure of his train, the packing of the two Gladstones was quickly accomplished and Janie and the children gathered quietly around. In an atmosphere of unnatural calm, Casey embraced his sons Charles and John Lloyd, aged twelve and four, and took his daughter Helen, then ten, in his arms. She buried her curly head on his shoulder, her little arms around his neck, and whimpered.

"I don't want you to go!"

"Papa'll be back soon, honey, and bring you a great big doll." Her father whispered in her ear, kissed her several times and put her down. His face bore a puzzled look.

Forcing a smile, he turned to Janie and found her with back turned and face buried in her hands.

"Sugarfoots!" He turned her around and took her in his arms, holding her tightly. She looked up and smiled through her tears.

"Remember, Casey Jones, be careful. And when your hand's on the throttle keep your eye on the rail!" He laughed.

"Jus' wait 'til we get settled in Memphis!"

Casey found his mother seated by the fireside alone.

"I thought you'd be by, my boy. I knew you were going to Memphis."

"Yes, Mother. You know this is what I've been lookin' forward to all these years."

Ann Nolen Jones smiled dreamily.

"I know." She said simply.

"And I want to remind you," continued Casey, "that if you and Papa ever need anything, just call on me."

"Don't worry about us, son. You've done your part already. We're getting along well enough. We're proud of you. No mother ever had a finer or more devoted son. When your father gets back from the school I'll tell him you called. Goodbye, Luther." She kissed him tenderly.

In the few remaining minutes Casey had time enough only to stop in at the division building and bid goodbye to his good friend, Train Dispatcher W. G. Eby, who, after telling him that Engineer Hatfield had given up his fast Memphis run, warned him to be careful, reminding him that his new run was the fastest and most dangerous on the system.

The last straw was laid on Casey Jones when just outside the division building he met Colie Chandler whose manner was unnaturally grave.

"Shake hands, Casey. I sure do hate to see you go over on that *Cannonball* run. I'll never see you again, old man. Goodbye."

But Casey shook it off with a grin.

"Goodbye, Runt."

They never met again.

CHAPTER XLI

THE CANNONBALL EXPRESS

MEMPHIS—a new home, a new locomotive and a new run. Engine No. 638 was past history insofar as her association with Casey Jones was concerned, and her former runner was now gazing upon an engine built for fast passenger service rather than heavy freight duty. She was a McQueen type locomotive and her number was *382*.

Engrossed in his inspection, Casey was not aware of the presence of any other person until he felt a slap on the back.

"So!" laughed the roundhouse foreman. "You just had to stop and look her over before coming to the office, eh? How d'ye like her, Casey?"

"Looks good to me, old timer. Where's my fireman, Sim Webb?"

"That's just why I wanted to see you at the office. As you probably know, you are assigned to runs 1 and 4 *Cannonball Express* with engine 382, alternating with Sam Tate on engine 384. Since you and Sim Webb are not familiar with track conditions between Memphis and Grenada, we are temporarily assigning you Tate's fireman, a negro boy named Lee, and placing Sim Webb with Sam Tate until he learns the road.   Then Sim'll be assigned regularly with you, and Lee'll go back with Tate."

Sim Webb was a colored boy distinctly above the average of his race in intelligence, character and general ability.   He had studied to become a doctor.   But the lure of the railroad caused him to give up the medical profession, and he had the good fortune while on the Water Valley District to fire many months for Casey Jones.   He felt that his highest ambition had been attained when he learned that he was to be assigned as fireman with Casey Jones on the Illinois Central's fastest run between Memphis and Canton.

It was in February, 1900, that Casey made his first regular *Cannonball* run, leaving Poplar Street station, Memphis, at 11:35 P.M., on time.   Down Beale Street, through South Yards and on into the open country, he sped with all the ease and assurance of a runner who had been familiar with the road for many years.   The fireboy, Lee, working furiously with the scoop, was tickled beyond description, and his admiration knew no bounds when he first heard the moan of No. 382's quill under the magic touch of the brave engineer.

Grenada—one hundred miles south of Memphis— and Casey was on home ground for the remaining eighty-eight miles to Canton.   He covered the entire 188 miles on schedule time; and likewise the return trip to Memphis, pulling No. 4 northbound *Cannonball*, was exactly on the advertised.

One of the hostlers at the roundhouse asked Fireboy Lee how he liked Mr. Casey Jones and the boy replied:

"Ah sho laks dat man. He sho can make dat whistle moan, but he sho am a *hard* Jack Driver."

On March 16th, 1900, Janie arrived in Memphis to spend a few days with Casey. She was at Poplar Street station to meet him upon his arrival on *Cannonball* No. 4, and at once suggested that they go to hear Dr. Talmadge, lecturer and evangelist, who was holding a revival in the Bluff City. Casey, surprised at such a liberal suggestion coming from Janie and fearing the consequences, offered a substitute suggestion. The result was that they went to a show instead, and next morning attended six o'clock mass. The rest of the day was spent in sightseeing and shopping and that night they attended the St. Patrick's Day ball at the Gayoso Hotel.

They had decided not to move to Memphis until May first, but late in April Janie returned to Memphis to hunt for a house. She wanted Casey to go with her, but he was busy with No. 382 and demurred.

"You go ahead and pick out a place, Sugarfoots. Whatever suits you suits me."

Meeting Casey at the Poplar Street station just before he pulled out on No. 1, Janie informed him that she had found just what they needed and that the family would join him about May first. They kissed each other goodbye, the last kiss, and Janie returned to Jackson.

Casey had previously written his friend, Fireman John Wesley McKinnie, telling him all about Memphis and complaining that Fireman Lee couldn't keep up the "kiyi" and that Sim Webb had been with Sam Tate ever since they came to Memphis. He urged McKinnie to join him. In the meantime, McKinnie, without advising Casey, had made up his mind to join his old pal as soon as possible, regardless of the opposition of the family.

CHAPTER XLII

THE END OF THE RUN

O N THE night of April 29th, 1900, Casey pulled into Memphis with train No. 4, on time, and was informed that engineer Sam Tate had been taken suddenly ill and would be unable to take out train No. 1. Although Casey was just in from the long run from Canton, he was asked to double out with train No. 1. He agreed at once.

Train No. 1, scheduled to leave Memphis at 11:35 P.M., was reported to arrive an hour and fifteen minutes late, which would make the actual leaving time 12:50 A.M. This was a long time for a fast train like the *Cannonball* to be behind the advertised. But apparently this circumstance gave Casey some measure of satisfaction.

The roundhouse foreman, noting the big engineer's pleased expression, observed:

"It's nothin' to celebrate over, Casey. You ought to be in bed."

"A fella," Casey returned lightly, "can crawl into bed any time. A whole hour gives us time to do things."

"What things?" asked the foreman.

"Well, Bud, this 382 hog o' mine needs as careful

ESTABLISHED 1869   REBUILT 1891

HOTEL TROLIO,

PETER TROLIO, Proprietor

RATES
$2.00 and $2.50
Per Day

Canton, Miss. 4 15 1900

Friend McK

I have been thinking
_____ _____ _____ _____
I wish you were over here with
me I have no partner now since
I left you If I had known
what I do now you would
have been here this is the
softest thing I ever went up
against you could hold it
just as easy as not I was
_____ _____ _____ _____
you did not come but after
I got all straightened out my
neigse had to go to court &
I had a white boy to it was
and easy for him & he is not
half as good a man on pienia

Casey Jones' letters to John Wesley "Bull" McKinnie.

HOTEL TROLIO,

PETER TROLIO, Proprietor

RATES
$2.00 and $2.50
Per Day

Canton Miss.

fller. as you are. I went out
to the race track the eth.
~~Saturday~~ or ~~Sunday~~ ...
the horses ... saw a ...
of things you want to tell
me. their be two miles
at the race track + they are
all fools and ... of the
stile in town dont ...
had an fuss + got sore ...
for all of this but a ...
~~I ~~ ~~coming~~ ...
up to come by granada +
go with me. if some of those
dummies dont tell what you
ask them write to me + I will
I dont know of any news that would
interest you now so good by
767 main str   Bayne

These are the only letters of record.

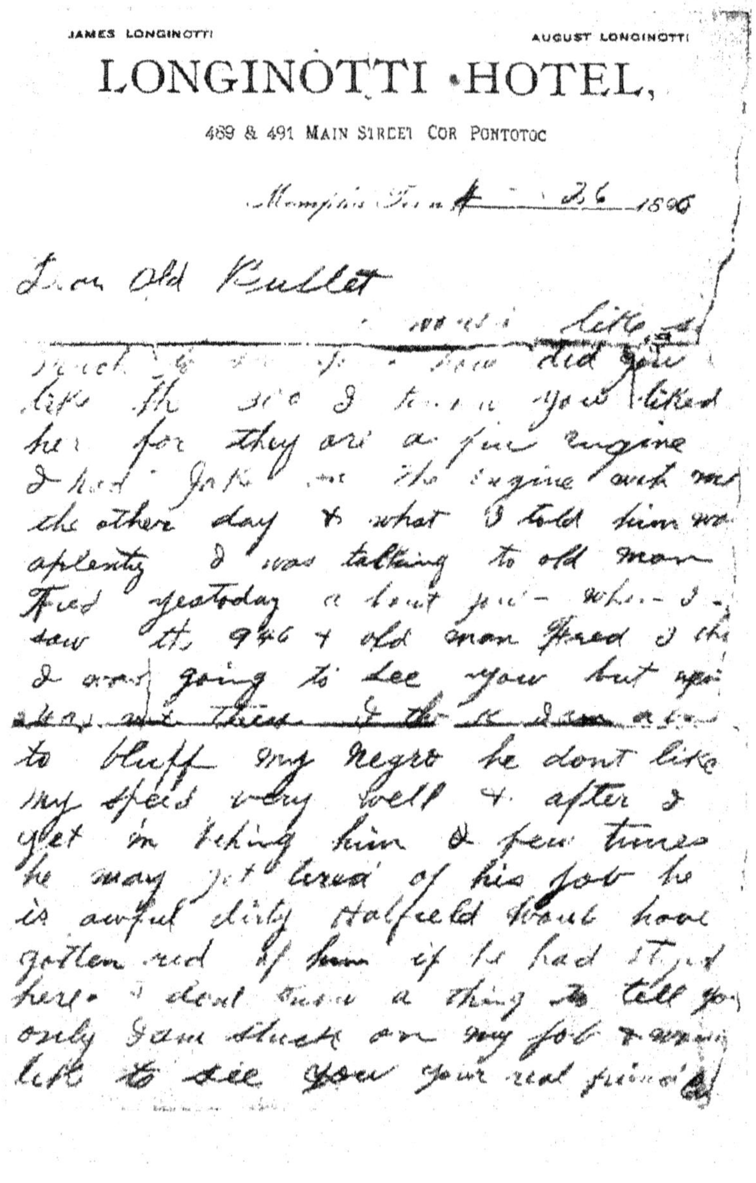

JAMES LONGINOTTI AUGUST LONGINOTTI

LONGINOTTI HOTEL,

489 & 491 MAIN STREET COR PONTOTOC

Memphis Tenn [illegible] 26 1900

Dear Old Bullet

[illegible] letter [illegible] did you like the 382 I know you liked her for they are a fine engine I had Jake on the engine with me the other day & what I told him was aplenty I was talking to old man Fred yesterday about you when I saw the 946 & old man Fred I thought I was going to see you but you was not there [illegible] to bluff my negro he dont like my speed very well & after I get in licking him a few times he may get tired of his job he is awful dirty Hatfield would have gotten rid of him if he had stayed here. I dont know a thing to tell you only I am stuck on my job & would like to see you your real friend

Casey Jones met his death four days after this letter was written

treatment as Maud S. She's just rolled in off her reg'lar run, and an hour's more time to go over her before takin' her out again means a whole lot."

"You don't mean—" the foreman began.

"Yeh, but I do." Casey took him up. "If I got to take No. 1 out when she's way behind th' advertised, it's goin' to be with my own jack, not somebody else's."

"You're crazy!"

"You're wrong, Bud. There's time to be made up, an' her an' me knows how to do it. Sam Tate's sick, so let his hog rest in th' stable while he's gettin' well."

The foreman reluctantly acquiesced.

This emergency brought together Casey Jones and his old fireboy, Sim Webb, for the first and last time on the Memphis run. Sim spoke up:

"You ought to be gettin' some rest, Mr. Casey."

"Not me, Sim," said Casey shortly. "When I was runnin' my ol' 638 hog, if we ever dragged into a terminal without havin' to double out, we thought th' road was ready to fold up. When this little lady here heads south tonight, she'll have her ears pinned back. We're goin' places!"

Sim groaned dismally, which elicited a laugh from Casey and the two hostlers who were helping with No. 382. Casey voiced an explanation of his fireboy's pretended dismay.

"Sim knows he'll have to give her plenty o' kiyi."

Promptly at 12:50 A.M. of April 30, 1900, Conductor Chap Turner of *Cannonball Express* No. 1

gave his engineer the highball, and the long train of twelve coaches pulled out of the Poplar Street station on what was to prove to be the most eventful trip of its history.

An hour and fifteen minutes behind time. Seventy-five minutes lost from a schedule that was already fast beyond what railroading today would recognize as safe!

How many of those lost minutes could Casey Jones salvage from the past?

Casey mentally ran over the 188 miles that lay between him and Canton. No. 1's running time for the entire distance was, regularly, about fifty miles per hour, and if lost time was to be made up No. 382 would have to be pushed up to sixty miles per hour, and much more than that over the best stretches. . . . And it was not a track over which one would crave to try for a speed record.

Casey had three scheduled stops to take into consideration. The first, at Grenada, would hold him eight minutes, while the other two—at Winona and Durant—ordinarily were little more than arrivals and departures. But once a train is behind schedule, it becomes the victim of all kinds of unexpected delays.

Then too, somewhere along the way he would have to meet No. 2, northbound *Cannonball*, and he only hoped that this would not delay him.

With this brief survey of the setting of the memorable run, the fact that *all but two minutes of the seventy-five minutes of lost time was made up in 174 miles*

attests the terrific speed at which train No. 1 traveled
that night. This means that there were times when
she was driving through the night considerably in excess of one hundred miles per hour, and hardly below
sixty-five miles per hour at any time!

At Durant, the last of the three scheduled stops,
where Casey had counted on getting in and out quickly,
his train was held for northbound No. 2, which should
have been at Durant in time to let him out without delay.

Roaring through the early morning hours, with the
nearer landscape flying past in a gray veil of night, only
one to whom the road was as familiar as the walls of
one's home could have had more than the vaguest sense
of location at any given instant.

Telegraph poles whizzed past like the pickets of a
fence. A cattle guard loomed dimly in the distance,
then came hurtling up the headlight's yellow beam
straight at the locomotive, only to be hammered and
ground under the spinning drivers. White mile posts
materialized ghostlike, far ahead, then catapulted at
No. 382 and swept past in a flash.

But to Casey Jones, every cattle guard, every mile
post, every dim landmark was as the page of an open
book. His hands left the throttle and airbrake lever
only when it was necessary to bear down on the whistle
cord. Folks along the right of way, snug in their beds
and only drowsily conscious, shot broad awake when
No. 382's whistle sent the mournful chime of the

whippoorwill call echoing across the wide countryside.

"Casey Jones! Doubling back south on No. 1. *And running fast!*"

Rapidly as the mile posts flashed past the cab, Casey identified each and every one of them with unfailing accuracy. This one was a signal to ease off a bit—soft track ahead. Another told him that it was safe to open up again. Another warned of a bad curve. Right there was where poor Dowling's hog left the rails and dived down the fill.—And so on, as mile after mile was ticked off.

Cool, collected, competent, Casey Jones automatically met every condition as it arose, and *Cannonball* No. 1 swept on through the darkness.

Back in the express and mail cars, messengers and clerks from time to time paused apprehensively in their work to marvel at the speed with which they were being hurled along. None had ever ridden so fast.

Passengers flattened their noses against the window panes and peered out into the dark. They could see nothing. But frequent applications and releases of the airbrakes, with accompanying jolts and jerks, and now and then an overpowering, uncanny sense of breathlessness, told them that they were being carried along faster than they ever had been before. When they attempted some light observation to conductor or brakeman, they met with no encouragement to chat. The trainmen went about their work silently, mouths grimly set.

SIM T WEBB
Portrait of Casey Jones' fireman on the "last run."

Sim Webb, in the gloom of the engine cab, was performing his allotted tasks as methodically as his hoghead—only he had never in many years of firing bailed so many black diamonds.   The night was chilly, but frequently he would have to pause and swab the sweat from his brown face.

At such intervals he would steal a glimpse of the image-like figure across the cab and dubiously shake his head.

Never had he seen Mr. Casey more assured, more himself.   If it were only daylight, Sim Webb reflected, how Mr. Casey would love to be watching the drivers roll! *

But despite the calm assurance with which the engineer stood—one hand on throttle, the other on the airbrake handle—watching the track ahead, Sim Webb apprehensively confided to himself:

"Mr. Casey's got a white eye."

Extreme fatigue of body and mind sometimes is responsible for the creation of the strangest mental and physical conditions.   There is a degree of fatigue wherein all sense of weariness and effort is inexplicably lifted up; wherein a feeling persists that one's endurance is boundless, and the brain seems to function with an alert, lightning-like vividness unknown to it in normal times.   It is akin to the morbid mental state said to be induced by certain drugs.   Yet the borderland between this acute state and fathomless sleep is defined

* See Appendix, note 5

by a hair's breadth. At the very moment of supreme effort, when one seemingly is never so wide awake and capable, drowsiness may unconsciously descend with incredible swiftness to cloud the faculties, and a strong effort of will may be necessary to fight off lethargy. It is a condition familiar to trainmen who have been obliged to labor until, almost literally, they have dropped in their tracks. And they have a name for it.

They call it "white eye."

Never had Casey Jones' mind been more alert; never had he known such a bouyancy of body. His thoughts raced on ahead of his train, then were suddenly occupied with incongruous incidents of a far away past; but all were as brilliantly clear as if etched in sunlight —a strange phantasmagoria.

. . . A night campfire in the woods. Tom Billingsby commenting on the boy who had never "sot eyes on one o' them thar trains o' steam cyars." . . . Sadie Carlisle lying stark in her own blood. . . . Emma's horrified revulsion at sight of the Mississippi. Ah, poor Sis! What a tragic end had been revealed to her childish eyes there upon the darkening river. . . . Janie playing the *Maiden's Prayer* and *Awakening of the Lion*. She seldom played those pieces any more; nowadays, when he was home, if she could find time to play at all, it would be *After the Ball*, *A Bird in a Gilded Cage*, *Just Tell Them That You Saw Me*. How scornfully she would refuse when begged to play the hoochie-koochie dance tune! Janie didn't believe it was a proper tune for a lady to play! . . .

Quite unconsciously he found that the hoochie-koochie tune was timing itself to the wheels clicking over the rail joints. Nobody had ever whistled or hummed the hoochie-koochie that fast!

Then the rhythmic clicking forced another monotonous repetition into his consciousness—over and over again until his brain reeled with it—*baled hay—shelled corn and baled hay*. . . . Again a feeling of pity surged through him, this time for the little black engine wiper. "He'll feel like hell when the gin wears off."

And then Durant.

With a shriek of brakes and a whistling of released air, train No. 1 made a quick stop at Durant—only thirty-five miles from Canton and the end of the run. No. 382's compressor was a pounding heart; she panted like a spent runner, recharging the air reservoirs. And the long train, straining as at a leash, was eager to plunge forward again.

The time was 3:28 A.M.; No. 1 had made up most of the precious lost minutes. Without further mishap the crew could count on pulling into Canton on time.

"Great work, Casey!" came the admiring voice of Chap Turner from below the engine cab.

But at once there arose an exasperating cause for delay; a detail which would oblige Casey to drive No. 382 the remaining thirty-five miles faster than ever before—if his purpose to make Canton on time remained unshaken.

The cause of delay was revealed by train orders and information which awaited *Cannonball* No. 1 at Durant.

The road to the south was almost blocked by a jam of trains at Vaughans,* a little station some twenty-two miles south of Durant and about fourteen miles north of Canton. Two freights had met at Vaughans, and there, before passing each other, were obliged to wait until three passenger trains had passed. These trains were, in the order of their arrival at Vaughans: No. 2, northbound; No. 26, a train of inferior classification, likewise northbound; and, lastly, *Cannonball* No. 1.

All this would have been simple enough but for one circumstance. The combined lengths of the two freight trains could not occupy the passing track without leaving two cars and a caboose hanging over on the main line track at either the north end or the south end of the passing track. In other words, *the switches at both ends of the passing track could not be clear at the same time*. And this necessitated what is known in railroad parlance as "sawing."

This sawing operation at Vaughans had delayed northbound No. 2, which, in turn, held Casey at Durant for two or three extra minutes—an additional and wholly unexpected delay.

* See Appendix, Note 14

Leaving Durant, Casey made a quick mental survey of the situation, and promptly decided that he could run the few remaining miles to Vaughans with the throttle pulled out to his chest. But tragic history was in the making and fate intervened.

Nobody could have foreseen that, at the most crucial moment, *an air line hose should burst on one of the waiting freights at Vaughans, locking the wheels and stopping the train dead!* *

Down into the blackness and fog roars *Cannonball* No. 1. The mile posts can not be seen so far ahead now. They materialize like wraiths in the headlight's yellow nimbus—plunge at the engine—flash past the cab—are swallowed up in the darkness. Switch lights are invisible until No. 382 is almost upon them. And they too flash past the cab and are gone. Underneath the wheels a rapidfire clatter tells how swiftly they are crashing over frogs and switch points. And the clicking of wheels over rail joints is like the ticking of Casey's watch.

Tick-tick-tick!

. . . shelled corn and baled hay—shelled corn and baled hay—shelled corn . . . The *ticks* staccato too rapidly for the phrases to be fitted to them; the words are getting all balled up. . . .

A white something shoots past the cab windows.

* See Appendix, Note 14

Seen through a haze of fog, it might be a tombstone in a cemetery. A tombstone running a fantastic race to meet No. 382.

But it can't fool Casey Jones; it is mile post No. 686. Only five miles more and No. 1 will be rolling past the switch at the north end of the Vaughans passing track.

Tick-tick-tick!

Shelled corn and baled hay—"shaled corn and haled bay" . . . Dern that crazy little nigger and his dreams! . . .

Five miles of good track. He can open her up to the limit and make those five miles in three minutes. Maybe less. Good little ol' 382! And then a quick slow-down to caution speed. The passengers might be jolted and shook up some, but No. 1 would be ready to be sawed through at the south end of the passing track. The fellows waiting there in the night mists and lonely darkness at Vaughans are all veterans, all old rails; they won't stick No. 1 a second more than necessary.

Another white tombstone dances past in the fog. Mile post No. 690.

One more mile.

A half-mile for a final supreme burst of speed. Another half-mile to bring the train down to caution speed.

It will be only a matter of seconds before No. 1 will be roaring out of the cut.

Then, so close upon him that he instinctively raised an arm to fend them off, the glowing red eyes of a

Courtesy Illinois Central System

Where Engineer James T. Gaffney broke into telegraph office to report the wreck.

caboose's rear lights grew out of the mist, glared savagely . . . plunged straight at Casey.

A strangled, horrified cry burst from Sim Webb. He heard Casey shout:

"*Jump, Sim!   Unload!*"

For the second time in the years that he was a hoghead, Casey Jones dynamited his engine. In virtually one motion, the throttle was thrust in, the Johnson-bar tugged into reverse, the airbrake lever shifted to emergency and the sand dome opened wide.

Yet Casey found time to bear down on the whistle cord to shriek a warning.

The terrific crash which immediately ensued jarred the countryside and was heard for miles around. The caboose was shattered to matchwood.

Scattering splinters and broken, twisted metal in every direction, No. 382's nose plowed into the next car, from whose wreckage dozens of bales of hay erupted, and on into the next car, showering tons of shelled corn over the right of way.

Then No. 382 tore loose from her tender, leaped a score of feet from the track and came to rest, drunkenly, with her smashed forward end pointing back the way she had come and to the havoc she had wrought.

Casey Jones lay dead among the wreckage, an iron bolt driven through his neck, a bale of hay resting across his body.

EPILOGUE

IT IS traditional that a captain must stay with his sinking ship and a locomotive engineer face certain catastrophe with hand on throttle and airbrake lever, devoting the last few moments of life to diminishing as much as possible the disastrous effects of an impending unescapable crash.

The heroic adherence to tradition of Casey Jones, when his locomotive plowed into the rear of a freight train at Vaughans that dark, foggy morning, was unquestionably the reason why many lives besides his own were not snuffed out, and why many persons were not maimed and mutilated.

In view of the terrific speed at which train No. 1 was flying, it is astounding that Casey so far succeeded in bringing it under control that not only was nobody else killed, but only two persons were even severely injured.

And of these two, Sim Webb, Casey's fireman, received his hurts as a direct result of jumping from the cab. He alighted among some bushes, ninety feet from the stationary caboose which the engine struck, and was incapacitated only a few weeks. The other casualty was A. J. Stein, express messenger on No. 1, who suffered injuries to his back and shoulders.

W. E. Woodson was foreman of a paint crew with

the work gang that was quartered in the camp cars at Vaughans. He was first to get to the dead engineer, and it was he who lifted a bale of hay from the lifeless body.

While Woodson, Engineer Bosma and others busied themselves at the immediate scene of the wreck, others of the various train crews hastened to the engine of train No. 26, in charge of Engineer James T. Gaffney. The telegraph office at Vaughans was closed and locked, and the men recalled that Gaffney was a telegraph operator as well as an engineer. This group battered in the office door, and the other carried the body to the station.

Gaffney called the dispatcher at Water Valley and notified him of the wreck and of Casey Jones' death, and was ordered to help clear the wreckage and assume charge of train No. 1 as engineer. As soon as the track was cleared, Gaffney proceeded to Canton with the train, conveying the body thither. Gaffney then ran train No. 4 north from Canton as far as Grenada, where he was relieved by Engineer Harry Norton.

And now came a striking manifestation of the affection which Casey's associates had for him. Unhesitatingly facing any hazard which their perilous occupation might offer, those men flinched at the notion of being bearers of the evil tidings to members of Casey's family. Particularly, they couldn't face Janie. The railroader of those days may have been hard-boiled, but in this crisis they showed themselves to have been amazingly soft-hearted. It devolved upon a woman, therefore, to break the news to Jane.

When the men one and all refused to accept the responsibility, the roundhouse foreman, Gus Franklin, appealed to a woman neighbor of Janie's, Mrs. Kate O'Hanlon, to shoulder the disagreeable duty. In appealing to Mrs. O'Hanlon, Franklin revealed a certain astuteness.

"It's a woman's job," he argued. "There's no man should even be looking at the little woman at a time such as this."

To which Mrs. O'Hanlon retorted: "Not the likes of you, at any rate. You're all a mighty poor lot to be thinking of yourselves as men."

Mrs. O'Hanlon drew her shawl over her head, framing her face, and, pinning it securely beneath her chin, resolutely set off to find Janie.

She found Janie in her yard with the baby, John Lloyd. The prescience of love read the dire message from afar. With her first view of the messenger one of Janie's hands fluttered to her breast and the other reached gropingly for the baby, as if instinctively seeking the comfort of actual physical contact with him. A pinched look settled about her mouth, and she saved Mrs. O'Hanlon the distress of trying to break the news by degrees.

"I know," Janie said quietly. "Casey is dead."

One might have gathered that she was not wholly unprepared for such a crisis, as if she had lived expecting

ROBERT ERNEST EDRINGTON

Who was "Ernest" to Casey Jones as he was and is to most of his
intimate friends   Mr. Edrington is Assistant Grand Chief Engineer of the Brotherhood of Locomotive Engineers.

it from day to day. It was Mrs. O'Hanlon who broke down and wept.

Thus it was that Janie first heard of Casey's death five hours and more following the accident.

The news came with brutal bluntness to Charles and Helen, the two older children, who were at school. During the forenoon recess a schoolmate, John Barry, was amazed by seeing Charlie Jones at school. John Barry exclaimed: "If *my* father had just been killed I wouldn't be at school!"

Charles and Helen were hard to convince of the truth. When they were, finally, they hurried home to their mother.

The funeral service for Casey Jones was held in St. Mary's church at Jackson, where he and Janie were married. Interment followed in Mt. Calvary cemetery. A newspaper account of the service names the following engineers as having been in attendance: P. J. Gaffney, C. E. Seiber, John E. Myers, Charles H. David, J. L. Kirby, B. H. Lashley, J. W. McKinnie, E. L. McCoy, W. H. Hartwell, J. L. Lewis, Peter Ohlson, C. M. Robertson, G. E. Krenkel, Arch McLeod and A. T. Rogers.

During his active career as engineer, Casey Jones was a member of Division 99, Brotherhood of Locomotive Engineers, at Water Valley, Mississippi.

APPENDIX

NOTE 1.—*Robert Ernest Edrington*

The enthusiastic cooperation of Mr. Edrington was of great assistance in the preparation of this volume.

Robert Ernest Edrington was born in Woodruff, Arkansas, on April 15th, 1883. After his father's death his mother returned with him to her former home at Water Valley, and the boy was only thirteen when he yielded to one of the most universal of boyish inclinations. He left home to strike out for himself.

Until the summer of 1898 he led the vague uncertain existence of an immature boy on his own, turning his hand to whatever offered to earn an honest dollar. During this period he found work successively as a baker, a tinsmith and a plumber at Greenwood, Mississippi. In the summer of 1898 he returned to Water Valley and obtained employment in the Illinois Central shops as machinist's helper. Here it was that he embarked upon his life's career.

During these tender years he attended public and country schools, supplementing his studies with attendance at night school and taking several correspondence school courses. He specialized in mechanical subjects, qualifying himself for advancement.

On February 23, 1901, less than three years after entering the Water Valley shops, he was employed as fireman on the Mississippi Division, and it is interesting to note that he started this part of his career on the famous engine 638, firing for Engineer Frank Newell who succeeded Casey Jones on this celebrated locomotive.

During the time that he was in firing service he held membership in the Brotherhood of Locomotive Firemen and served as Local Chairman Firemen's Lodge #402, Water Valley. On January 31, 1904, he was promoted to engineer and became eligible for member-

ship in the Brotherhood of Locomotive Engineers one year thereafter. On December 20, 1921, he was elected Chairman of the
General Committee of Adjustment, Brotherhood of Locomotive Engineers, Illinois Central System, and after serving a full three year
term as General Chairman, was unanimously reelected for a second
term of three years, but when former President Stone passed away
in June, 1925, was elected Assistant Grand Chief Engineer by the
Advisory Board and was elected for a six year term by the 1927
Convention in Cleveland, Ohio, and still holds the same position.

Under date of September 25, 1931, Mr. Edrington addressed a
letter to Mrs. Jones, from which the following is quoted:

"The writer when between fifteen and sixteen years of age secured employment at the Water Valley shops as machinist helper in
the roundhouse, at which time 'Casey' Jones was regularly assigned
to freight engine 638, running between Water Valley . . . and
Jackson, Tennessee, which at that time was known as the Jackson
District of the Tennessee Division. I distinctly recall . . . that
your husband had become famous as an engineer, especially among
Illinois Central employees and was referred to by all as 'Casey' . . .

"Practically all repairs on engines . . . were made in the Water
Valley shops; moreover, as engineers were assigned to regular engines, they manifested personal interest in repairs and upkeep to the
greatest possible degree, spending a considerable portion of their
time during layover periods in the roundhouse at Water Valley in
personally following up and seeing that repairs they had reported
on forms provided for that purpose were made by the shop forces.
Naturally, all roundhouse employees became well acquainted with engineers in this manner, and as Casey perhaps displayed more interest
in the upkeep of his engine than any of the other engineers, obviously
he spent more time with the shop employees, which resulted in a
closer acquaintance between him and the roundhouse employees than
between other engineers and these same shop employees.

"In many sections of the United States and Canada I have listened
to the song 'Casey Jones'; also have read so many articles in the

press and magazines that were inaccurate in discussing the life history of 'Casey,' the man whom I as a boy placed on the very highest pedestal, that I have despaired of changing the universal opinion undoubtedly formed as the result of the song created in the mind of a simple negro roundhouse employee of Canton, Mississippi, who was among the many who loved 'Casey' and cherished the memory of their acquaintanceship.

"My conclusion with respect to Casey, both as a man and a locomotive engineer, based upon my close observation of him, is that he was unexcelled in faculty of making and retaining friends, temperate in all habits, exceptionally high class morally; also recognized by the management of the Illinois Central as possessing unusual and outstanding qualifications as a locomotive engineer."

*　　*　　*

NOTE 2.—*John M. Taylor*

Mr. John M. Taylor, in 1933 Vice-president of the Johns-Manville Company, adds his tribute to the memory of Casey Jones in a letter written to Mrs. Jones on October 24, 1931. In 1893 and for several years thereafter Mr. Taylor was chief clerk in the master mechanic's office at Water Valley. The following paragraphs are from the letter referred to:

"I recall the feeling that went over me when the telegram was received at our office at Water Valley advising that Casey Jones, who was beloved by all his co-workers, had been killed with his hand on the throttle.

"Casey was also beloved by the management because of his loyalty and ever ready spirit to answer the call of duty. He was not a shirker or fairweather engineer, but responded promptly to the call in all kinds of weather, dark and rainy, sleet and cold—all the same to him. He was genial, kind-hearted and of a lovable disposition. We hear of heroes in various walks of life. Casey's tragic death but shows the heroic side of his life."

NOTE 3.—*B. J. Feeny*

A letter from B. J. Feeny, written October 5, 1931, contains some interesting data. Mr. Feeny is a past president and present executive member of the Traveling Engineers Association (1934) and also an active traveling engineer of the Illinois Central. In 1930, when the association held its annual meeting in Chicago, Mr. Feeny presented to the gathering Sim Webb and Mrs. Jane Brady Jones.

"I was running a locomotive on the Kentucky Division contemporary with Casey," Mr. Feeny writes, "with whom I was personally acquainted. I made many extra trips into Memphis and remember . . . many of the circumstances of the ill-fated trip of Casey Jones . . .

"On the ill-fated trip, Casey Jones was running Engine 382, afterwards changed to 212, 2012, and 5012."

Mr. Feeny wrote subsequently, October 27, 1931:

"In my last letter to you I quoted numbers of engine Casey Jones was running, and Sim Webb states they are as follows: The engine number was 382 on which Casey was killed, later changed to 212, then to 2012 and now is 5012."

*   *   *

NOTE 4.—*Change of Gauge*

It would be interesting to know whether the construction department of any present day railway company is prepared to perform the extraordinary feat accomplished by the Illinois Central back in 1881, when it changed its main track between East Cairo, Kentucky, and New Orleans, a distance of 561 miles, to standard gauge in the incredibly short time of *a little more than three hours!*

August 1, 1881, was the date. Only the most able generalship made the performance possible. Everything from the Ohio River to New Orleans was in readiness for the "zero hour," waiting for the signal to start. At the appointed time work commenced simul-

taneously.—Main line traffic was delayed considerably less than four
hours. Samuel E. Matthews, deceased Illinois Central Conductor of
Jackson, Tennessee, was one who participated in the gigantic undertaking.

*   *   *

NOTE 5.—*Put in your water and shovel in your coal—*
        *Put your head out the window and watch them drivers
        roll.*

These lines from the popular version of the *Casey Jones* ballad
strike a true and characteristic note. "Riding in the engine with
him, as I often did," writes A. J. Thomas of Fort Worth, Texas,
"and seeing him watch his drivers roll, I recall this as typical of
Casey Jones."

*   *   *

NOTE 6.—*Starke Letter.*

Mr. Claude M. Starke, in 1933 a successful business man of
Chicago, was for thirty-six years connected with the Illinois Central
Railroad Company in various capacities. For seventeen years he
served as master mechanic at different places on the system. In
1893, when a boy, Mr. Starke was a clerk in the master mechanic's
office at Water Valley and, according to his own testimony, a devoted admirer of Casey Jones. During the subsequent years Mr.
Starke has continued to cherish the memory of one who was a hero
of his boyhood days. On October 11, 1931, commenting on his
pleasant memories of Casey Jones he wrote as follows:

"I am delighted to tell you of my association and acquaintance
with him, beginning in the summer of 1893, when I secured my
first job of railroading.

"Like most of the boys in Water Valley, Mississippi, I had often
watched Casey pull out of Water Valley, northbound on 52 for Jackson, Tennessee, and the next day Jim McClendon—or 'Crip,' as he

was known to his cronies. These two had the fast freight run out or northbound, and returned on what I afterward learned to be 55, which arrived some time after midnight.

"Our baseball ground was located near the yards, and whenever Casey arrived with his hog . . . the ball game would be called until his caboose disappeared going over the hill. Even so you could hear him whistling as he got his train under way, going through Cathey's cut and through Springdale bottom. I am sure that every farmer along the line knew as well as did our baseball club when Casey was on the run and on time.—It was always both with him, as he seldom laid off and did not know what being late meant.

"Mr. George Dickey was master mechanic in Water Valley at that time and John M. Taylor, (See Note 2, *supra*) now a vice-president of the Johns-Manville Company, was the chief clerk in the master mechanic's office. Through Mr. Taylor's influence I secured a job as night clerk in the same office in mid-summer of 1893.

"The office was equipped with a board to which all of the through wires could be plugged in, and it was customary for the day force to receive and send all messages pertaining to the mechanical department, direct. There were no telephones in those days. The first night or two I was there I looked at the board and wondered what it was all about, but would not have dared to pull out or change one of the plugs for the world.

"I had many duties assigned to me, one being to make out copies of all stock reports; therefore when one of the engineers who arrived on my shift had killed an animal, they had to come over to my office and make out their reports.

"It was not long before I learned that Casey arrived on 55 around four o'clock; but as he had not yet killed anything, it was several weeks after I was employed that he had to come over.

"I shall never forget when he walked into the office and said: 'Bud, let's make out a stock report. I killed a heifer, coming down Waterford tonight.'

"I knew him, of course, the minute he walked into the office. He sat down and I handed him the blank to fill out. Said he:

" 'You go ahead and make it out. I'll tell you what to put in and will sign it.'

"So I read the many questions—many of them seemed foolish—and each answer he gave would make me laugh. At last it was made out, he sitting there all the while with his long legs crossed and upon the desk.

"After it was finished, I was loath to let him get away, and began to talk to him about his trip down, and so on. He did not seem in any hurry to get home, and I learned that his family lived in Jackson, Tennessee, and that he boarded at Mrs. Block's, which was near the roundhouse, and that he always waited until after breakfast before going to bed.

"After a while it was time for me to get the office in shape for the day forces, so he got up to go. As he started out of the office, I invited him to come back the next trip in. He asked me: 'Do you think I'm going to kill another heifer?' At any rate, he did come back the next trip and many afterwards. He found that my office was a more comfortable place to wait until time to go to break-fast than in the roundhouse office.

"Shortly after his first visit, and no doubt on the first, he noticed the telegraph sets in the office and the board (switch-board) with all its plugs, that I would not have dared touch. He asked me if I knew anything about telegraphing. I replied that I did not. He went over to the board, and much to my horror began pulling out and pushing in plugs, moving them about here and there, as a re-sult of which the instruments on the desk began clicking off the messages going over the various wires.

"He stood there listening intently to the messages, frequently making remarks to me about their importance, etc. After he had tired of this, he would put the plugs all back in their proper places and the instruments would become silent.

"Then he would tell me about when he was an operator. Many times when he had the board cut in, he could not resist grabbing the sending key and 'talking' to an operator on the other end of the line. You see, this was before the days of block signals and almost every siding had an operator. He knew them all on his district, and would get a big kick out of talking to them from the master mechanic's office.

"One morning when he was visiting me he said: 'How would you like to learn to telegraph?'

"I was just crazy to, as most kids are, and said so. He said:

"'All right. If you will string up the wires from here over to the roundhouse office, I'll see if I can get some instruments and teach you Morse.'

"Needless to say that I got the wires up all right. And sure enough, he came in one morning and had instruments for both offices. He helped me install them, connect up the batteries, etc., and pretty soon we had the sets going. There was another boy in the roundhouse, and we gave him the alphabet and got him interested. My call was SO. To this day I can remember it (... . .) and on the mornings when Casey came in on No. 55, I could hardly wait to hear him call me from the roundhouse office.

"In the meantime I had laboriously picked out messages to send to him. It was only a matter of two hundred yards from one office to the other, and when he sent me a message and I didn't answer promptly, he would stick his head out the window and shout to ask me what was the matter. Then he would come over and give me a 'lesson.'

"This went on for several months, in which time I got to know Casey very well indeed, and when not busy I would go down to the cinder pit and wait for him to come over from the yards and go with him up to the roundhouse office to make out his work report, register, and tell the night foreman what he wanted done to his hog—which he insisted be kept in first-class condition.

"After a while I was put in the machine shops to learn a trade. I missed Casey dreadfully for a while and used to wonder if he didn't me. Pretty soon I was interested in building locomotives instead of watching them go by, and when it was his turn to go out on No. 52, I would slip away to the outbound track and have a few words with him before his departure.

"During the time I was working in the office at night, I shall never forget the circumstances surrounding his arrival on No. 55, which was around 3·30 A.M. At this hour of the morning it was always still, and sound could be heard miles away. All the old darkies would be listening for 'Mr.' Casey. Miles away in the north you could hear Casey blowing his whistle, telling everybody that he was coming in and that he had made a safe trip. The old darkies would begin to croon and moan with his whistle, and it was from them that many of the verses about him originated. I recall the names of many of these colored boys: Andrew Crockett, Gid Miller, Wilson Glover, Bob Davis, John Visor and many others, all of whom were great admirers of 'Mr.' Casey Jones.

"As time went on, Casey's seniority gave him rights on the Memphis-Canton run, where he met his death.

"For years, many of the colored firemen on the Mississippi Division insisted that when they passed the spot where he was killed they could hear distinctly the warning whistle that all was not clear."

*   *   *

NOTE 7.—*Wallace Saunders*

The genesis of the *Casey Jones* ballad is easy to trace. Wallace Saunders was just such a Negro as the text portrays: ignorant, unlettered, extremely simple-minded, a typical representative of the class of darkies legion in the Black Bottom country of Mississippi.

But Wallace did possess one natural gift—an extraordinary talent for extemporizing words and tunes and fitting them together; and in the same manner as the songs of medieval minstrels and troubadours were passed along from person to person, so did Wallace's creations gain currency and circulation.

One of Wallace's ballads has surpassed all his others. It contained that indescribable something which gave it both popularity and permanence. It is the song *Casey Jones*.

Long before the practically identical tunes *Steamboat Bill* and *Casey Jones* were given the permanent form of printed words and music, thousands of individuals were familiar with the words and melody of Wallace Saunders' *Casey Jones*,—the original version. *Steamboat Bill* need not be considered here further than to call attention to the marked resemblance of its tune to the Wallace Saunders creation.

There was an engineer on the Illinois Central in the year 1900 and for several years thereafter whose two brothers constituted a team of vaudeville performers, constantly alert to pick up new songs, new jokes, new gags—anything that might make a hit with the public. The engineer's name was William Leighton. The brothers were Bert and Frank Leighton, and their attention was directed to the possibilities contained in Wallace's crude ballad. The Leighton Brothers sang a version of *Casey Jones* in various theatres of the country, adding a chorus.

In 1909 a song *Casey Jones* was published by T. Lawrence Siebert and Eddie Newton, the former being credited with the lyric and the latter with the music. The lyric wandered far afield, but the melody corresponded to the one sung by the Leighton Brothers and was a close approximation of the original melody.

Some time after Casey's death when the song began to be hummed, whistled and sung—the performers using such words as they could recall or themselves improvise—several of Casey's friends began to urge Wallace to give them the words to the ballad as he sang them so that they could be permanently transcribed. Wallace, mysterious and reticent, steadfastly refused until Engineer John R. Gaffney coaxed him with a bottle of gin. The words of the original ballad by Wallace Saunders follow:

Come all you rounders if you want to hear
The story told of a brave engineer;
Casey Jones was the rounder's name,
A high right-wheeler of mighty fame.*

Caller called Casey about half-past four;
He kissed his wife at the station door,
Climbed into the cab with his orders in his hand,
Says, "This is my trip to the Holy Land."

Through South Memphis yards on the fly,
He heard the fireman say, "You got a white eye."
All the switchmen knew by the engine's moan
That the man at the throttle was Casey Jones.

It had been raining some five or six weeks;
The railroad track was like the bed of a creek.
They rated him down to a thirty-mile gait—
Threw the southbound mail some eight hours late.

Fireman says, "Casey, you're running too fast.
You ran the block board the last station we passed."
Casey says, "Yes, I believe we'll make it through,
For she steams better than ever I knew."

---

* If one of the early unwritten versions were followed the last line of the first stanza would be transcribed to read: *"On a six-eight wheeler he won his fame."* No such monstrosity was known in railroading, however, as a "six-eight wheeler." On the other hand, there is nothing cryptic about the phrase *"high right-wheeler."* For a railroad man to be called a "right-wheeler" by his co-workers—or, with warmer enthusiasm, a "high right-wheeler"—meant that he was given the stamp of unqualified approval and admiration.

Casey says, "Fireman, don't you fret.
Keep knocking at the fire door, don't give up yet.
I'm going to run her till she leaves the rail
Or make it on time with the southern mail."

Around the curve and down the dump,
Two locomotives were bound to bump.
Fireman hollered, "Casey, it's just ahead!
We might jump and make it, but we'll all be dead!"

'Twas round this curve he spied a passenger train.
Rousing his engine, he caused the bell to ring.
Fireman jumped off, but Casey stayed on.
He's a good engineer, but he's dead and gone.

Poor Casey Jones was all right,
For he stuck to his duty both day and night.
They loved to hear the whistle and ring of No. 3
As he came into Memphis on the old I. C.

Headaches and heartaches and all kinds of pain
Are not apart from a railroad train.
Tales that are earnest, noble and grand
Belong to the life of a railroad man.

Wallace clearly took some liberties with the facts; in some instances, obviously, to fill in or find a rime. But the verses, in the main, bear abundant evidence that he was familiar with the true circumstances.

The word "rounder" as applied to Casey must be taken as a light, affectionate appellation, as Wallace Saunders used it. "Rounder" and "boomer" were commonly regarded as synonymous, and Casey, either as fireman or engineer, never rode a locomotive on any railroads other than the Mobile & Ohio and the Illinois Central. He was the antithesis of what the word rounder implies.

The retention in their version of "rounder" by Seibert and Newton, and their adoption of a far western background, suggests some interesting speculation centering about Casey's younger brother, Frank, who railroaded in the West, was sometimes called "Casey," and who may be described correctly as a rounder or boomer railroader.

*   *   *

NOTE 8.—*Throttle Device*

Various of Casey's contemporaries mention a throttle attachment which he invented and installed in Engine 638, which gave him a hair-line control of power and speed. From attempts to describe the device one infers that its principle depended on a system of gears which enabled the engineer to manipulate the throttle lever with micrometric adjustments. It seems not to have appealed to engineers generally, Casey apparently being the only one who utilized it.

*   *   *

NOTE 9.—*Major E. S. Hosford*

Major Hosford is still held in pleasant remembrance by many persons who knew him during his active railroad career. Especially are recalled his friendly attitude toward subordinates—the rank and file under him—and his amiable, kindly disposition. Mr. B. B. Tolson, superintendent of the Mobile & Ohio Railroad at Murphysboro, Illinois, writes under date of November 28, 1932:

"In 1879 Major E. S. Hosford was division superintendent at Jackson, Tennessee. His division extended from Tupelo, Mississippi, to Columbus, Kentucky. After the Mobile & Ohio was extended to East Cairo in 1882, and in 1886 had acquired the St. Louis & Cairo Railroad—Cairo to St. Louis—the former Jackson Division and Major Hosford's position were abolished. Major

SIM WEBB

Although retired, rides the cab of the famous "Panama Limited"
between Memphis and Canton, Miss. in the Fall of 1938.

Hosford then entered the service of the Illinois Central at Jackson, Tennessee, and became Claim Adjuster. He has been dead for a number of years."

* * *

NOTE 10.—*Beauregard Hamilton Lashley*

Beauregard Hamilton Lashley or "Bose," as he was more intimately known among his many friends and acquaintances, had a long and distinguished career as locomotive engineer, first on the Mobile & Ohio and later on the Illinois Central. His close friendship with Casey Jones made him a valuable source of information.

Retired from active service, Mr. Lashley lived at his home in Jackson, Tennessee, until his death on March 20, 1935.

* * *

NOTE 11.—*Sim Webb*

Under date of December 6, 1931, Sim Webb, Casey's fireman on the "last run," wrote to the author as follows.

"Mr. Jones and I were working out of Water Valley and we were chosen for the run out of Memphis. We temporarily were assigned separately due to the fact that neither of us was acquainted with road conditions on the Memphis District. I was placed with Mr. Sam Tate and Mr. Jones was given a fireman already familiar with the Grenada District."

Relative to Casey's last run the letter continues: "That trip had been very successful up to the time of the accident. We had gotten the train one hour and fifteen minutes late out of Memphis. The engine was functioning perfectly and we were making up time, and would have gone into Canton on the minute, as we were only two minutes late when we had the wreck, which happened at 3:52 o'clock."

* * *

NOTE 12.—*No. 638's Whistle*

This historic whistle, whose distinctive sound inspired in its hearers such descriptive phrases as "the call of a whippoorwill" and "the war cry of a viking," was kept by Engineer P. J. (Pete) Gaffney for many years. Later it was found in his tender box and restored to Mrs. Jones.

The whistle and Casey's watch are among the treasured mementoes of her famous husband now in her possession. The hands of the watch indicate that it was stopped at eight minutes to four—or, in the idiom of the road, at 3:52.

*   *   *

NOTE 13.—*The Chandlers*

Edgar Chandler, the oldest of the four Chandler boys, was born in 1861, and served successively as switchman, fireman and engineer on the Illinois Central. He died in June, 1897, after a service record of seventeen years. His widow, Mrs. Belle Chandler, and two daughters, Edna and Jewel, still reside in Jackson, Tennessee.

Lee Chandler started out as call boy on February 15, 1882, became fireman on March 1, 1884, and engineer February 2, 1888, which position he continues to hold, *having perhaps the longest continuous service record of any active railroader in the United States.* He is now in his fifty-eighth year of service—fifty-six years on the "smoke end," four as fireman and nearly fifty-two as engineer! Now in his seventy-sixth year, he is assigned to the classy Seminole Limited run over the division between Cairo, Illinois, and Jackson, Tennessee. His first wife was Marguerite McColpin and they had four children, Ruth and Marguerite, both deceased, and Robert and Edith, both living. Lee Chandler remained single for thirty-one years after his first wife's death. On December 23, 1929, he married Belle Hearn of Martin, Tennessee. They reside happily at Jackson, Tennessee.

Paul Chandler entered the Illinois Central service in June, 1887, as call-boy at East Cairo, Kentucky. He became fireman on June 8, 1889, at the age of eighteen years, and was promoted to engineer January 20, 1895. *He has a continuous service record of fifty-one years* and is one of the oldest engineers in seniority on the entire

GOLD SERVICE AWARDS

Presented to Lee Chandler and Colie Chandler by L. A. Downs, President of the Illinois Central System, at the Stevens Hotel, Chicago.

system. Since 1915 he has served as engineer on the crack Panama Limited between Cairo, Illinois, and Memphis, Tennessee. Paul Chandler married Bettie McDade, now deceased, of Fulton, Kentucky; and they had two children, Bera who died in infancy, and Thomas who still lives with his father.

Colie Chandler began his career with the Illinois Central as engine wiper in 1887, became fireman October 3, 1890, and was promoted to engineer on December 9, 1895. His service is continuous for the past fifty-two years and he is likewise among the oldest engineers in seniority on the entire system, serving now on the Seminole Limited run, the same as his brother, Lee. He was married in Dresden, Tennessee, January 16, 1897, and there were eight children, seven of whom are living,—Eddie, Charlie, Mable, Nell, Grace, Hazel and Flo,—all residing at Jackson, Tennessee.

Such, briefly, is the amazing service record of the Chandler brothers. The family is traditionally a railroad family. The father of the four brothers was Carroll A. Chandler, born February 15, 1836. He married Mary E. Griggs in 1859 and there were two daughters in addition to the four sons. Carroll Chandler entered the Illinois Central service as clerk on the railroad ferry H. S. McComb at East Cairo, Kentucky, in 1879, and although his service record totaled only ten years, it marked the beginning of one of the most interesting family histories in the annals of the railroad. The two daughters of Carroll Chandler were Mrs. Lilly Person, wife of engineer Walter Person, now deceased; and Mrs. Molly Hunt, wife of traveling engineer Tom Hunt, both deceased.

Eddie F. Chandler, oldest son of Colie, served the Illinois Central as caller and roundhouse clerk during a period of more than ten years. Charles, the other son, served the Illinois Central from May 7, 1916, until December 24, 1919, as caller and flagman, then transferred to the Mobile & Ohio with which company he now holds a position in the roadmaster's office.

Colie Chandler and his wife and children are an interesting family group, keenly intelligent and witty. In the field of enter-

tainment they have been compared to Eddie Foy and his seven little
Foys.   Mrs. Chandler and the seven children formed a vaudeville
troupe several years ago and played in numerous important towns
throughout the southern states.   Mrs. Chandler was the accomplished
pianist and director, Eddie and Charles were end men in the min-
strel, Mable was interlocutor and able performer on almost every
known musical instrument, while the four other girls (Nell, Grace,
Hazel and Flo) were talented singers and dancers.   Hazel and Flo
have been featured in many broadcasts over important radio stations.

"Papa" Colie is a great sports enthusiast.   He hasn't missed a
World Series in thirty years and has witnessed nearly every running
of the Kentucky Derby since the turn of the century.   Among his
friends in the sport world are B. B. Jones, whose box he shares at
Churchill Downs, and Judge Kenesaw Mountain Landis, High Com-
missioner of Baseball, who has ridden with him in his engine cab.
Referring to her father's trip to the 1939 Kentucky Derby, his
daughter Grace Chandler writes as follows:

"Papa and Charlie have just returned from Louisville where they
saw the race.   They had a good time, Papa pulling very strongly for
Technician, which horse, as you know, made a very poor showing.
But as Al Jolson says, 'Why establish a precedent this year?'   Poor
Papa always loses!"

Joe Pitts of Sharon, Tennessee, pays the following rhymed tribute
to Colie Chandler:

ON TIME

There's a little engineer
    I've known mos' all my life
He's as wild about his engine
    As he is about his wife
He sleeps down at th' roundhouse
    Same's he does at home
But his sleep all put together
    Would 'mount to almos' none

One mornin' he came rollin' down
   A little after eight
I listened for th' whistle
   He was a little late
But soon I heard him comin'
   Th' fireman had her hot
For the 'leven sixty seven
   Sure did th' Turkey Trot

As he sailed 'round th' curve
   Down th' long old Sharon hill
He squeezed her jus' a little
   'Till she set her trailers still
When he crossed th' Dredge Ditch trestle
   There beside th' water tank
He gave her two more notches
   And th' throttle one big yank

Then he spoke up to his fireman
   Said "I know this job is old
But to do this thing in style, boy,
   You mus' give her lots o' coal"
Then he eased down on his cushion
   With th' pride that each one has
While th' monkeys did th' Motion
   And th' drivers did th' Jazz

Now she slipped right on to Greenfield
   Up that old four mile hill
Near th' crossin' folks could hear him
   Do th' "Toot Toot" with th' quill

Then he passed th' Greenfield station
  But he had to slow her down
That was jus' a little rulin'
  Of that one an' only town

When he swings on into Milan
  There's a red light on th' gate
He's a funny little fella
  Never likes to run 'em late
Then he leaves this little station
  Knowing well it's his last stop
The fireman starts to jam her
  'Till th' steam begins to pop

Down th' line thru "Old Medina"
  Right off down th' Birdsong Hill
Five more miles of speed an' danger
  Gives th' folks on board a thrill
Jus' nine more miles to travel
  'Till he gets a bite to eat
In nine minutes he mus' make it
  If he reaches Chester Street

But he said "Ah, that's a picnic
  If I ever get to heav'n
I can vouch to old St. Peter
  That I made it once in seven"
As he rolled up Union Station
  A smile was on his face
He eased on down to Chester Street
  With dignity and grace

Then on down past th' Gas House
Where he makes th' whistle moan
That's a signal to his wife and kids
That he will soon be home
And his pal, "Old Sixty-Seven"—
Th' train was Number Nine
Ten sleepers and two baggage cars—
They pulled right in on time

His name is Colie Chandler
He has a lovin' wife
He's a reg'lar railroad man
And has been all his life
If they ever build a railroad
All th' way from here to Heav'n
Th' first man out is Colie
On th' 'Leven Sixty-Seven

On May 4, 1939, the author called on Lee Chandler and his gracious wife and had a delightful visit, being most royally entertained. Although in his seventy-sixth year and long since eligible for retirement, Lee was just as youthful and enthusiastic as ever. When asked how much longer he intended to run an engine, he smiled and replied: "Until I'm a hundred." He then proudly exhibited a certificate of the company doctor, dated the previous day, attesting his physical fitness for continued active service.

After hours spent in reviewing dramatic incidents, the comedies and tragedies of the past, the author came away more convinced than ever that here was one of the most amazing characters in the history of the railroad.

*   *   *

NOTE 14.—*The Situation at Vaughans*

At the time of the wreck at Vaughans there was one passing track 3,148 feet long used for meeting and passing trains. There was also a house or storage track for loading and unloading cars.

On the passing track was northbound freight No. 82 with fifty empty cars, with Engineer William Bosma, Fireman Kennedy, Conductor J. R. Hoke and Flagman Ed Crawford as the crew; also a southbound double-header extra with twenty-seven loaded cars, with John Markert, engineer of the pilot engine; Ed Hoke, conductor; and Bailey Newberry, flagman.

These two freight trains had four cars more than the capacity of the side track could accommodate, which necessitated a "sawing" process in order to make a clearance for trains passing through on the main line. The first train to let pass at Vaughans was northbound express No. 2, which stopped between the switches until the two freights could saw it by. This caused a delay of two or three minutes to northbound No. 2 and likewise to southbound No. 1 at Durant, where these two fast trains were to meet.

With No. 2 on its way to Durant, this left the north end of the passing track clear, and apparently all was in readiness for southbound No. 1, Casey's train. But in the meantime, northbound local passenger train No. 26 arrived at Vaughans for No. 1 to pass, and this necessitated another sawing process, the southbound freight backing out on the main line and the northbound freight following it until No. 26 could head in on the house or storage track. Train No. 26 was in charge of Conductor P. B. Wilkerson and Engineer James T. Gaffney.

After No. 26 had cleared the south switch and was at rest on the house track with markers turned, the northbound freight immediately started backing out on the main line a sufficient distance for the southbound freight once more to pull in far enough to clear the north switch for No. 1.

What then occurred would not happen again under similar circumstances in perhaps a millennium. An air hose burst on the fourth car behind the engine of northbound freight No. 82, freezing it to a dead standstill and likewise blocking the southbound freight which had three or four cars hanging out on the main line at the north

end in the face of the onrushing No. 1.   Before fireman Kennedy
could apply a new air hose, the crash came.

*   *   *

NOTE 15.—*Six Hundred Class Locomotives and First Runners*

CAIRO DIVISION

Engine	Engineer
601	"Big Foot" Brannon
602	Colie Chandler
603	Dixie Fenner
604	Frank Hughes
605	Ed Rarick
606	Hugh McDonald—Eugene Jones
607	Mike Mulvoy
608	Ed Chandler
609	Tom Hunt
610	Andy Devlin
611	Lee Chandler
612	John Baxter—Paul Chandler
613	Albert Meriwether
614	Tom Weldon
615	Will Watkins
616	Charlie Steelman
617	Ed Powers
618	S. S. Wooley
619	Garrett Perry
620	Archer Burr
621	Lee Merritt

WATER VALLEY DIVISION

622	P. J. Gaffney
623	W. E. Leach
624	Frank Foss

WATER VALLEY DIVISION—(*Continued*)

625 . . . . . . Frank Love
626 . . . . .John R. Gaffney
627 . . . . .John Kirby
628 . . . . .John Morehead
629. . . . . . J. E. Myers
630 . . . . . Tom Haines
631. . . . . . Tug Markert
632 . . . . . . William Hatfield
633. . . . . . .Archie Smith
634. . . . . . .Sam Tate
635. . . . . . .W. R. Ruffin
636. . . . . . .J. Boone
637. . . . . . .Bose Lashley
638. . . . . . Casey Jones

*   *   *

NOTE 16.—*Memorial at Cayce, Kentucky*

On Sunday, October 9, 1938, a crowd of several thousand people gathered together at the little town of Cayce, Kentucky, to witness the unveiling and dedication of a monument in honor of Casey Jones. Senator Alben Barkley of Kentucky sang the praises of the famous engineer in delivering the principal dedicatory address, referring to Casey as a "real hero" and a "peaceful" man who gave his own life to save that of others. He described the memorial as an "unusual honor to an unusual man in an unusual way."

The memorial was promoted by the Hickman Lions Club with the assistance and cooperation of citizens of Cayce, Fulton and other communities and the donations of friends and admirers of the noted engineer. Mrs. Casey Jones was present with her son Charles, her daughter Helen, and two grandchildren. Many distinguished guests attended.

U. S. Senator Alben Barkley delivering the dedicatory address at Cayce, Kentucky.

CASEY JONES

IN THIS COMMUNITY
THE FAMOUS LOCOMOTIVE ENGINEER
JOHN LUTHER JONES
ALIAS CASEY JONES
SPENT HIS BOYHOOD DAYS

CASEY JONES

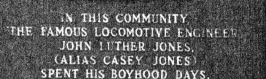

IN THIS COMMUNITY
THE FAMOUS LOCOMOTIVE ENGINEER
JOHN LUTHER JONES,
(ALIAS CASEY JONES)
SPENT HIS BOYHOOD DAYS.

CASEY'S MANY RECORD FEATS AS LOCOMOTIVE
ENGINEER ENGROSSED HIM DEEPLY IN THE HEARTS
OF HIS FELLOW WORKERS. ON THE MORNING OF
APRIL 30th 1900, WHILE RUNNING THE ILLINOIS
CENTRAL FAST MAIL TRAIN NO.1 "THE CANNON BALL"
AND BY NO FAULT OF HIS, HIS ENGINE BOLTED
THROUGH THREE FREIGHT CARS AT VAUGHN, MISS.
CASEY DIED WITH HIS HAND CLENCHED TO THE
BREAK HELVE AND HIS WAS THE ONLY LIFE LOST.
FAMOUS FOR BRAVERY AND COURAGE, THE NAME
OF CASEY JONES LIVES DEEPLY SET INTO THE
HEARTS OF AMERICAN PEOPLE IN BOTH TRADITION
AND SONG. IT CAN BE TRUTHFULLY SAID OF HIM
GREATER LOVE HATH NO MAN THAN THIS THAT
A MAN LAY DOWN HIS LIFE FOR HIS FRIENDS.

ERECTED BY ADMIRERS OF CASEY JONES JULY 9th, 1938

CPSIA information can be obtained
at www.ICGtesting.com
Printed in the USA
BVOW10s0044301117

501339BV00002B/37/P

9 781376 332773